D1064196

THE
VIEW
FROM
SECTION
111

BY MIKE SHATZKIN

PRENTICE-HALL, Inc.
Englewood Cliffs, N.J.

ISBN 0-13-941831-8

Library of Congress Catalog Card Number: 78-129506

Printed in the United States of America   T

Prentice-Hall International, Inc., London
Prentice-Hall of Australia, Pty. Ltd., Sydney
Prentice-Hall of Canada, Ltd., Toronto
Prentice-Hall of India Private Ltd., New Delhi
Prentice-Hall of Japan, Inc., Tokyo

Far below the bottom of an orange bowl
are two baskets and a hardwood floor,
20,000 colored seats
and 20,000 people filing in.

We have all met before.
In Macy's.
In voting booths.
On opposite sides of tear gas in the streets.
Everyone forgets.
There is another war we are waiting for.

The athletes are warm.
The anthem is sung.
The play is about to begin.
I know
nothing else could have brought us together.

Jack Litewka

CONTENTS

Introduction	vii
October 2	1
October 6	4
October 9	6
October 15	11
October 21	14
October 23	17
October 29	21
November 13	25
November 16	28
November 22	31
November 25	34
November 29	38
December 2	41
December 9	43
December 11	46
Darrall Imhoff	51
December 16	56
Donnie May	59
January 23	63
Bob Wolff	69
February 3	76
February 8	80
Johnny Warren	90
February 17	95
Willis Reed	102
March 8—Boston Garden	108
March 17	112
March 19	116
March 24	121
March 30	124

April 6 128

J. Walter Kennedy 131

April 8 136

April 14 140

April 21 145

April 26 151

April 29 157

May 2 160

May 6 166

May 8 173

May 9 176

The Game Itself, Including

Hints on Terminology 182

Offensive Basketball 185

Defensive Basketball 190

The League Structure 194

Introduction

As a Knick fan, I revel in their first championship, achieved last night. As a citizen of a country increasingly tormented by racism and violence, intolerance and insanity, I sometimes have trouble justifying to myself an endeavor such as this book. It may provide pleasure to some, but I sometimes wonder if it will help solve any of the problems that threaten our existence. In the long run—and I can only hope this is not purely a rationalization—I think that we must start with the things that can bring us together if we are ever to eliminate the pressures that pull us apart as human beings. I think a happy public is less likely to kill and destroy than an unhappy one, and sports brings happiness to more people in our society than anything else, save love.

I met a lot of people in Section 111 during the course of the season who would never have been known to me had we not shared the Knickerbockers for this wonderful season. Some of us hit it off well from the very beginning—indeed, my friendship with Dan and his wife Roz will extend to the next Knick season, when we plan to buy seats together again. Some of us did not hit it off so well at the start, a fact perhaps rooted in the prejudices others entertain for people with long hair, or perhaps based on my sometimes thoughtless distrust of suited, well-groomed members of the establishment. In the end, however, I think we are all friends, and that is what is really important. I have been reached by thoughts that have nothing to do with basketball, and I hope I have had success reaching others during the conversations we have had during times-out and halftimes. I sometimes think that if the leader of the SDS and the burly construction workers who went on a rampage in New York yesterday could be forced to sit through half-a-hundred Knick games together, they would also be friends, though perhaps not in agreement.

I would like to thank all those with whom I shared this season for helping to make it the enjoyable experience it was. I would also like to apologize for any bad thoughts expressed about them throughout this book. There were times we didn't get along, but what is important, as I said, is that we are now friends.

I also owe a debt of gratitude to Bob Wolff for the encouragement and advice he so generously offered from the day I met him last January right up to the present. A couple of days ago we discussed the strike on college campuses that has grown out of the Cambodian involvement and he was as concerned and sincere as he is in his support of the Knicks or Rangers. I like to think that he is not alone in the Knick organization or in sports.

Most of all, I must thank the Knicks. They provided me, and countless other basketball fans, with much more than victory. They symbolized the accomplishment of unity, with the tacit understanding that the parts can all be different in makeup if they contribute to a better whole. There is a lesson in that for all of us.

I shall not ask you to keep in mind while reading this book that there is war, racism, repression, and violence in this country. This book is about the Knicks. What I shall ask is that when you finish this book you do not forget that the Knicks can be a beginning of peace, not just an end to a championship.

Mike Shatzkin
New York City

THE
VIEW
FROM
SECTION
111

OCTOBER 2

Fall is really coming. The football season is far enough along that what has happened is significant: the Colts were bombed by the Vikings, the Jets lost both their games and some defensive players on the last two Sundays, the Cincinnati Bengals have won three games in a row. We are wondering who will be playing in the World Series. But in New York—where paved playgrounds are the most prevalent recreation areas and kids grow up throwing round balls at metal hoops rather than oval balls at other kids—the most prominent sign of fall is that basketball, 1969–70, is almost here.

The New York Times seems to carry something every day —box scores of Knick exhibition games seldom appear but there is news, and they're winning more than they're losing. The *Post,* perhaps not as good a paper but superb in basketball coverage, has much more copy, and the news is good. Dave Stallworth is apparently healthy again two years after suffering a heart attack that should have ended any thought of playing basketball again. Walt Frazier—"Clyde" to his teammates and fans—is stealing the ball, passing, and shooting just as he did in the glory days last winter. Johnny Warren starred for St. John's—and it looks like he'll stick with the Knicks. Cazzie Russell's ankle is healthy again. Phil

Jackson isn't ready to play yet but he's shooting the ball—maybe he'll come back too.

The local unveiling is this Saturday night at the Garden; all the Knick exhibitions so far have been on the road. This weekend, though, Lew Alcindor will come to town with what was last year a ragtag Milwaukee Bucks team but this year will be a contender. The whole division is going to be topsy-turvy. The Celtics have lost Bill Russell, which leaves them primarily with John Havlicek and Celtic pride. The Philadelphia 76ers seem demoralized—both Billy Cunningham and Luke Jackson may be playing out their NBA string, Chet Walker was traded, and Hal Greer is another year older. Legs do not age like fine wine and Knick fans know this. We all hope that Dick Barnett still has a season or two of spring left.

The Bullets should be stronger than last year, simply because everyone is returning and has a year's more experience with his teammates. Cincinnati has to be helped by the coaching of Bob Cousy. With Oscar Robertson and Jerry Lucas anchoring the team, they don't need much more. Detroit might be the most improved team in the Eastern division. Jimmy Walker has lost weight, Walt Bellamy will be playing with his new teammates from the start of training, and everybody—but everybody—can shoot. Bill von Breda Kolff is a capable coach, and without the personality problems that Wilt Chamberlain engendered with the Lakers, could enjoy a long and successful tenure at Detroit.

There will be plenty of fans on hand for the curtain-raiser, which is also Alcindor's first professional appearance in New York. This town loves basketball, and this is the beginning of the new era in professional basketball. In keeping with the era in New York sports just begun by the Jets and the Mets, the Knickerbocker fans this year expect to win it all.

I know there will be plenty of fans on hand, because this game is included in the season-ticket package—a precaution that hardly seems necessary to sell the seats. By the time I got my season-ticket application, one month ago and six weeks before the opening of the season, every decent seat on side court was sold out for the season. The choice was "cheap seats" or "end line." I chose "end line," and will find out Saturday whether to cry about the $294 it will cost me to sit there this year.

I've been a Knickerbocker fan for many years—since the days of Gallatin and Sears, Braun and Felix. We always lost, but I always went—end-promenade tickets at the old Garden cost $2.50 then. Ten years later they're called "court" and they cost $6.

My devotion to the Knicks does not provide the only reason for this book. I went to college in Los Angeles, and during the past four years I've been to the Sports Arena and the Forum tens of times as well as listened to Chick Hearn broadcast countless Laker games. Compared with the basketball environment in which I was raised, it seemed that Los Angeles fans were fickle and unknowledgeable. Southern California fans come to games late, leave early, and bring portable radios to have Hearn explain to them what is happening before their very eyes. They cheer every player in a Los Angeles uniform and show little appreciation for the visitors—except in extraordinary circumstances, such as for Sam Jones on the occasion of the last game he played in Los Angeles (which was, incidentally, also the last game Bill Russell played there). I remember it as being different here. I hope to find that it is as I remember it.

I also hope that the ballplayers feel that way. There has always been discussion about the unfortunate star ballplayers who did not play in New York and consequently were not recognized as they might have been. Perhaps this is true of Roberto Clemente and Henry Aaron in baseball. Is it true also of Zelmo Beatty? Is it true of Jeff Mullins? Could it be true of John Havlicek or Jerry Lucas? I hope to find out, and in doing so find out what they think of us as fans.

3

Most important, I hope to find out who the New York Knickerbocker fan is, what he thinks and feels about basketball. What does he talk about while entering the Garden? And what does he talk about as he leaves? Does he accept victory as gracefully as he has historically accepted defeat? And how will increased victory affect his acceptance of occasional defeat?

I was very young when I decided that having season tickets to the Knickerbocker games was a worthwhile dream. Now that I've realized it—at least for this year—I want to milk it for everything it's worth.

OCTOBER 6

My seats are at the very fringe of the $7 section—people only a few rows behind me are paying $1 less per game, $42 less for the season. Still, the seats are good, not too high and straight off the corner of the floor. I won't complain about the seats.

However, I might complain about the basketball if the Knickerbockers continue to play as they did on Saturday night. Their performance, which earned them a sound trouncing by the Milwaukee Bucks, was totally uninspired and uninspiring. Nobody really played very well: Frazier didn't penetrate, DeBusschere didn't rebound, nobody shot well, and—much to the chagrin of some St. John's fans who chanted for him—Johnny Warren didn't even play.

Milwaukee is not a very good team, although with Lew Alcindor in the lineup, I imagine they'll win some and possibly make the playoffs. Flynn Robinson scored 40 points with a nicely balanced shooting performance of bombs, drives, and jump shots. Jon McGlocklin, Milwaukee's other guard, scored 22, mostly on long jumpers when the harrying Knick defense left him alone on one side of the court. But neither man was particularly effective at getting the ball in-

4

side to Lew, even after Willis Reed picked up four fouls in the first quarter and Bill Hosket came in to guard him. (Nate Bowman had a bad hand and did not suit up.) Hosket tried to play in front of Alcindor, generally difficult strategy for a man giving away half-a-foot in height to execute. Milwaukee's only good passer, Guy Rodgers, was on the bench at the time Reed was out (and played very little with Alcindor).

If this constituted poor coaching on the part of Larry Costello, it didn't help the Knicks. They weren't hitting, but more important, they were not getting inside shots or offensive rebounds. DeBusschere was making Milwaukee's Don Smith look like an all-star. I doubt that he will be, although on Saturday night he was the most solid player on the floor.

Stallworth, in his first Garden game since his heart attack a year and a half ago, was quick and showed no signs of ill health. However, he was victimized by the bad game his teammates played. For an individual Knick to look good on Saturday night would have been a Herculean task.

The game was dull, but my neighbors were most interesting for their diversity. On my right was a quiet man who looked like he was from Long Island. (It is difficult to explain or justify that characterization—it's a feeling you get when you are a New Yorker who is not from Long Island.) He brought his wife to the game and was discussing some of basketball's finer points with her. In front of me was a shaggy-haired couple I would have expected to find at some of the other places I frequent—the Fillmore East or the Bitter End. I don't know if they'll be there for every game, but if they are they qualify as the People Around Me Who Most Likely Would Make Interesting Company. We didn't get off to a good start. My loud and constant concern over the Knicks' poor play apparently affected the young lady's ears, and her beau had to ask me to tone it down. He was quite polite about it, and it was obviously not something he relished doing.

On my left was a family of five—if they're going to be at every game they've spent $1,470 for basketball this winter. They would have to be quite the fans. However, season-ticket-splitting may be a common phenomenon. A man in back of me was talking about meeting this Sunday with his partners to decide which of them were going to what games this year. It is also entirely possible that many of the fans around me will not be back at all. I'm sure that many who bought season tickets used this exhibition game to be generous and treat friends and relatives to a ballgame before things get serious.

The crowd was not a sellout, nor was it very noisy. There were few moments that warranted any crowd excitement. When the Knicks made a brief stir at the close of the first half, so did the fans. When the locals closed the gap to 83–69 with 2½ minutes to go in the third quarter, there was some handclapping and whistling. But it was to no avail. The final score was 120–104.

The Times noted briefly (among long stories of Jet, Met, and Giant victories) this morning that the Knicks beat the Russell-less Celtics last night for a 4–2 exhibition record. I hope the omen for the season lies in that performance, not in Saturday night's. The season starts next week with four games in five days—Seattle and Los Angeles at home and Cincinnati and Chicago on the road. Because of a miserable start, there was no championship last year. Maybe this season the Knicks can postpone the slump—until June!

OCTOBER 9

Starting as early as I discovered professional sports—somewhere around the second or third grade, and extending well past grammar school—I amused myself by preparing elaborate sports predictions: pennant winners, batting averages, scoring and rebounding records, even individual game play-by-plays for mythical all-star teams. My heroes always did admirably. Duke Snider, and later Roger Maris and Mickey Mantle, compiled fantastic home-run records and never batted less than .320. The Knicks always won the playoffs in October, with Richie Guerin, Kenny Sears, and Carl Braun never dipping under 20 points a game. Jim Brown always ran for 300 yards, Andy Bathgate always scored 3 goals and had 5 assists (2 or 3 to Andy Hebenton, who played on a different line).

By the end of the season, these papers were always lost, fortunately for my prognosticator's ego. But, being a grown fan now, I feel confident that I can put aside the dreams of what would be nice and really discern what should be. So I am making predictions in this entry and swearing to myself that they will appear in the book as I write them now— no matter if Emmette Bryant leads the league in rebounds and Fred Crawford in scoring.

The Knickerbockers will win the Eastern Division in a tight race, but in a convincing fashion. They will do so for two primary reasons: speed and depth. Willis Reed will be the only consistent high scorer; he'll probably average close to 25 a game, with Frazier at about 20 and DeBusschere at around 18, but Walt's scoring will come in bursts of 40 points a game and dips to 10. At least two men on the bench will be in double figures: Cazzie Russell and Dave Stallworth; and Donnie May and Bill Hosket will develop to the point that one might be traded for a guard by the middle of the season, depending primarily on what kind of return they warrant.

The only other clear choices in the East are that Cincinati will finish sixth and Boston last. The Royals have Robertson and Lucas for openers, but not enough else. Connie Dierking is an adequate center, but there are far too many much better than he, including the centers on the five teams that will place ahead of the Royals in the East. Oscar, for all his skills (and nobody has more), is a pouting kind of ballplayer who will have trouble getting along with Bob Cousy. Lucas has aching knees and may be losing interest—he gave far too serious thought to retirement to convince me that his heart is really in the game anymore. Tom Van Arsdale came on, but he is still not as good as Adrian Smith was, and he is about the last good player Cincy has. Maybe Cousy can work a miracle.

Boston, for the time being, has had it. John Havlicek may be the premier ballplayer in the NBA, but he cannot carry the team. The Celtics may come close to .500—they would be a threat in the West—but I see no way for them to pass anybody in the East. Bailey Howell is older, Emmette Bryant is older, Satch Sanders is older and often hurt. Larry Siegfried's style of play will be badly affected by Russell's absence, as will Havlicek's, but Havlicek will shine anyway because he's so good. If the Knickerbocker fans must learn to be gracious winners, the Celtics' followers have the opposite lesson to learn. Maybe the ballclubs should just switch franchises!

On paper the Baltimore Bullets look second-best in the East. Their starting five (Martin, Unseld, Johnson, Loughery, and Monroe) is magnificent, and their bench is strong. They can run, rebound, score, and play defense. But they are not quite as good as the Knicks. With New York and Los Angeles, however, Baltimore is in the league's elite.

Philadelphia probably has enough to beat out Milwaukee and Detroit for third place if Luke Jackson is really healthy again and Hal Greer can still top 20 points every night. Wally Jones and Archie Clark are the best pair of second guards in the league, but neither is good enough to replace Greer if he loses his speed and touch. Billy Cunningham is one of the best forwards in basketball, but he has an eye to his future in the ABA, a fact that cannot be lost on his teammates, his fans, and his performance; all will suffer. And somebody will have to pick up some scoring slack for Chet Walker, no matter how underrated his replacement, Jim Washington, is.

The toughest race will be between Detroit and Milwaukee for the last playoff spot. Detroit has a bevy of shooters with a history of losing. Milwaukee has Lew Alcindor at center, Flynn Robinson to score, and an awful lot of hope. For no particular reason, I think Milwaukee will take the fourth spot. Here sentimentality may govern. I went to UCLA with Lew, I know him casually, and have followed him avidly. I find it hard to believe that there's much he can't do, including leading Milwaukee to the playoffs.

The West won't be close. It might have been, if Rudy LaRusso hadn't retired and Rick Barry been denied to the Warriors. It might have been, if Zelmo Beatty hadn't decided to sit this year out, denying the Hawks a center who could have neutralized Wilt Chamberlain. But it won't be now—Los Angeles, the team of Elgin Baylor, Jerry West, and Wilt, as well as Jack Kent Cooke and the Fabulous Forum, should make it a runaway.

San Francisco will finish second on the strength of two men, Nate Thurmond and Jeff Mullins—with a little help from their friends. Heaven help the Warriors and my predictions if either Thurmond or Mullins is hurt very much.

Atlanta will finish third because they have a great coach (Richie Guerin), good shooters, and hustling defenders. Lou Hudson will pick up in his scoring, partly because he's getting better and partly because he'll get the ball more with Jim Davis replacing Beatty in the middle. Walt Hazzard and other fine Atlanta guards can move the ball inside, and the Hawks will seldom beat themselves.

Phoenix will finish fourth, but they'll have a battle with San Diego to make it. The Suns are strengthened considerably by three additions: Connie Hawkins and Jerry Chambers at forward, and Neal Walk at center. Hawkins, so they say, can do it all. Chambers had a good start with the Lakers before he went into the Army. He can shoot and is quick. He may not start at the beginning of the season, but he will come along. Having a player of Dick Van Arsdale's size and defensive ability at guard—freed to play there because of the addition of Hawkins, Chambers, and Paul Silas—will help Gail Goodrich immensely.

San Diego has no guards, sadly enough for Elvin Hayes, John Block, and Don Kojis, who comprise one of the league's best front lines. The Rockets will breathe on the Sun's backs, but they will finish out of the money.

Seattle and Chicago will bring up the rear of the West. The Sonics need a couple more ballplayers, but they have a nucleus. Lucius Allen will someday be a great one, but perhaps not this year. Bob Rule will score and score but he does not get enough rebounds, and even with Coach Wilkins in the backcourt, Rule will not have enough help.

The Bulls are well-coached by Dick Motta, but simply too weak. Jerry Sloan is a solid pro and Chet Walker can score. But Clem Haskins leaves much to be desired defensively at guard and their 7-foot center, Tom Boerwinkle, doesn't seem to be good enough.

This will be a classic season. It may be the last one for Laker greats West and Baylor. Jerry must someday reach the breaking point on broken noses, and Elgin is finding the seasons getting longer and longer. Jerry Lucas, as noted earlier, has already contemplated retirement. The Knicks and Bullets are going to emphasize what was commenced last year—that the balance of professional basketball power has shifted to them. Big Lew will make a Big Splash.

And lest I forget—the Knicks over the Lakers in the NBA finals. There may be a touch of wishful thinking here, but every sports fan has a dreamer in him.

OCTOBER 15

The season opened in a blaze of glory, and it is clear that whatever the Knicks were looking for ten days ago against Milwaukee was found when they played Seattle last night. They were devastating.

Going to the Garden last night shook loose a lot of memories that had been locked in nooks and crannies, far corners of the brain. You can enter the new Garden on an escalator that delivers you from a quiet terrace overlooking Pennsylvania Station to a madhouse lobby. People are busy dashing for ticket lines to see "what's left for tonight," vendors hawk programs, banners, yearbooks, pictures, and all the other paraphernalia that make the price of the ticket only the down payment for a father treating a son to a ballgame. High school lettermen in emblazoned jackets wander through the lobby discussing their sports and their leagues and their exploits with their friends, focusing only occasionally on what they are about to see. Before you reach your seat it is certain that someone will comment that he saw Willis Reed (or Bill Bradley or Dick Barnett) walking on Eighth Avenue yesterday. You, of course, have never been so lucky.

I found my seats without an usher this time. One advantage to having season tickets is that you save the 25¢ tip that Garden ushers almost demand for showing you to your seat. Over the course of the season that amounts to $10.

Again the Garden was not full. Indeed, there were empty seats below me that must belong to season-ticket-holders. Maybe the interest in the Mets (who won today to lead the World Series, 3–1) is so great that some basketball fans are waiting for the end of the Series to start attending. Maybe some folks want to start their season with a good club—the Los Angeles Lakers will be here on Saturday. It seemed like there were more empty seats than there were for the Bucks' exhibition.

The man to my right wondered whether I was "writing again this week." I explained I'd be taking notes at every game. That opened him up. After hearing that I had not been around for four years, he extolled the new Garden crowds and told me how excited and crowded it would get as the season progressed. The organist ran through a four-note marching riff from time to time, and I was told that later on in the season the crowd wouldn't let him stop playing it. Better that than the National Anthem, I guess.

The Knickerbockers commanded the ballgame from the first quarter. Bill Bradley got them off on the right foot, pumping in four jump shots in the opening period. After he cooled off, Frazier, Barnett, and Willis Reed got hot and the Knickerbockers led by more than 20 at the half. The defense was brilliant—particularly Frazier, who was stealing passes and dribbles and leading the fast break like a pickpocket on a motorcycle. Bob Rule, Seattle's most solid ballplayer, led the scoring at the half with 17 points, having had good success with an outside jump shot and with quick moves around the basket. Reed led New York with 14 despite a long rest in the second quarter, while Barnett had 13 and Frazier and Bradley 12 apiece. The balance was indicative of the Knicks' strength. They were hitting the open man, penetrating for good medium-range jump shots and layups. They did not do that against Milwaukee. Of course, they were not playing against Lew Alcindor.

Lucius Allen, whom I watched as a freshman and for two varsity years at ULCA, played about 20 minutes. My new friend on the right (in more ways than one!) informed me that Lucius was a "dope-addict"—referring to the marijuana arrests that Lucius, through his carelessness, had incurred. I imagine he would have been shocked to know that among UCLA athletes, Lucius's primary distinction had been that

12

he was caught. Allen was nervous, but skillful. He made a couple of good passes and drives and showed the ability to hit the jump shot off a quick move that served him so well in college.

In back of me, at halftime, a man was reminding his friends that the "Knicks are playing a very weak team." He repeated it several times. And it was true. But it is also true that the Knicks played well enough last night to beat anybody, and that Seattle will not be so weak as the season progresses. They are young in the pivot and at guard (except for Coach Wilkins), but solid at forward. They will get tougher and better. Of course, it will be some time before they are capable of a performance like the Knicks gave last night. It won't come this year.

Dave Stallworth got a standing ovation of some duration from the crowd when he was announced before the game, and he saw plenty of action. Dave the Rave is definitely back. He swirled around the court like a Wichita tornado (which he is) and showed an outside shot that is better than I remembered. Johnny Warren also got to play and did creditably, although he missed some open shots. His quickness on defense, however, indicates that a substitute for Frazier—when he is tired or in foul trouble—may be in the making, and he could be ready later this year.

Nate Bowman gave the only really sorry performance of the evening. He committed an "up-and-down" traveling violation when he had an unmolested 10-foot jump shot on a fast break, fumbled some passes, and threw the ball away. The crowd, friendly to Nate under better circumstances, nearly laughed him off the court and gave him a facetious standing ovation when Holzman pulled him for Billy Hosket. My friend on the right bluntly labeled him the "worst back-up center in the league." The other side of that coin, as far as the Knicks are concerned, is that Phil Jackson was announced before the game and they are still hoping he will be back this season. Jackson, also a solid cornerman, would be the best back-up center in the league.

If the Knicks could play like they did last night every night, they would finish the season 82–0. But they can't, of course and they have a rough game tonight on the road against the Royals. The real test of the infant dynasty, however, will be this Saturday night when they face the Lakers (their fourth game in five days). If things are looking as bright on Sunday morning as they are today, the Knicker-bockers could be stealing as much attention from the Mets in April as the Mets are from them now.

OCTOBER 21

Saturday night's game against the Lakers, which the Knicks won, 99–96, was like a playoff game. It was the kind of exhibition that any pro-basketball fan would hope for on a night he was taking someone to a game to convince him that pro basketball is the best spectator entertainment in the world. The pace was furious, the individual performances by Jerry West, Willis Reed, and, in spots, Dick Barnett, Elgin Baylor, and Dave Stallworth were overshadowed only by the brilliant teamwork. Both teams opened up big leads and both teams fought back furiously from behind. The game was like a war with a series of battles for which there was a distinct winner and a distinct loser. Saturday night's game was a classic.

And it should have been. The Garden was almost full—most of the gaps were in the expensive seats, which doesn't bother the management, because they were sold to season-ticket-holders months ago. As already mentioned, the Knicks and Lakers constitute, with Baltimore and perhaps Philadelphia, the class of the league. Jerry West is the best shooter in basketball history, Wilt Chamberlain the greatest all-

14

time scorer, and Elgin Baylor—in my opinion—the most outstanding basketball player that ever lived. Baylor's skills are dimming now. He is still capable of plays that no other human can even describe, let alone emulate, but they do not come as frequently as they once did. These plays, however, still come only from Baylor.

The Knicks came into the game 3–0, having knocked off Cincinnati and Chicago on the road following the opening-night win at the Garden over Seattle. Cincy, coached by Bob Cousy, fought tough, but the Chicago game was a romp. The only question was whether the Knicks might be tired playing their fourth game in five days. The Lakers had lost their only game, to Philadelphia, the night before.

I still thought that I might become friends with the fellow in front of me, but it seems less likely now. He went on a quiet diatribe before the game, complete with big words and sarcasm, asking me to tone it down since we had to sit a row apart for the entire season. At this point, things like that can't bother me too much. When I was a kid, I was bought peanuts three different times at Yankee Stadium by wealthy box-seat customers who wanted to shut me up for an inning or two. (To their chagrin, they found I could go through a bag of peanuts during one Yankee rally. But that was in the Mantle and Maris days.)

From the opening tip, the game was very rough, but there was little fouling. The Lakers clearly had the better of the play in the first quarter, as Chamberlain and Mel Counts combined to limit the Knicks to one shot per downcourt trip, and the Lakers constructed a 27–19 lead by the buzzer. There was no real feeling of concern among the multitude about the deficit. Frazier was handling the ball well and penetrating, and this is generally the key to the Knicks' success. Reed and DeBusschere are rarely shut off the boards for a whole ballgame, even by a pair of 7-footers like Chamberlain and Counts.

15

And, indeed, things changed shortly into the second quarter. Dave Stallworth got hot after the Lakers had moved to a 38–30 lead and led the Knicks back to a 45—44 advantage. The teams went off the floor for the half tied at 49, and the rumbling at the beautiful new Madison Square Garden Center was reminiscent of older rafters and younger days just a few blocks uptown.

The Knicks jumped from the starting block for the second half, this time with Dick Barnett supplying the punch. Four and a half minutes into the stanza the 8-point advantage (60–52) was leading East, with Barnett scoring 9 of the Knicks' 11 points.

During that sequence there occurred a play that was indicative of the Knicks' teamwork, the key to their success. DeBusschere, freed by several picks at the foul line, passed up a 15-footer to give Barnett a 20-foot jumper. Dave knew that Dick had the hot hand. That is they way the Knickerbockers win.

The Lakers fought back to within a bucket by the quarter's end, 73–71, only to have the Knicks come swinging off the fourth quarter bell to again build up a big lead. But the Lakers refused to quit, and, with Jerry West (who scored 42 points) leading the revival, they pulled close for the final minutes. Chamberlain missed a crucial foul shot near the end, probably the only mistake the Lakers made down the stretch. (It was a smart Knickerbocker play to foul him as Wilt is a poor foul-shooter. Both in the head and on the ball, the Knicks were equal to the task.)

I discovered two real characters at this game—whom I hope I will not see again. A loudly dressed middle-aged man two rows below me gave it to the referees after almost every call in language suitable for a football locker room. During a second-quarter time-out he turned around and loudly apologized to all the ladies present whom he might have offended. He slipped away before the start of the second half and a woman took his seat next to the lady he'd escorted. I can only assume that two couples were pooling seats and that the men decided at halftime not to bother to educate the ladies at the expense of their own enjoyment of a very serious ballgame. At least to this fellow, it was a serious affair.

The other was a man behind me who played "I am very well-informed" with his family and, for the most part, did fairly well. However, he completely blew it when he explained the "1-and-1" foul situation, giving them the college rule that "if you make the first, you get the second." In younger days I might have turned around to correct him. Being older and wiser—and facing the wrong way to know just how big he was—I decided to live with his mistake. But only as long as it took me to write it down.

The ballgame represented one very important milestone for the Knicks. It was not just their fourth win to start the season. It was not just a victory over a great team that took all but one game from them last year. It was not just a great team victory or a great defensive showing. It was evidence that the time is here when the Knicks won't scare. They can see a lead dwindle and not throw what remains of it away. They can hang on against tough teams when things get sticky. This was the hallmark of Bill Russell's Celtic teams, who might frequently have been saved by the bell (as they were in the final victory for the championship last spring), but who knew that they had really saved themselves. Another four-games-in-five-days grind starts tonight at home against Phoenix, but this time the Knicks know they can do it. They have finally started a season off right.

OCTOBER 23

Well, the season is about 6 percent completed and the Knickerbockers are undefeated. Tuesday night's game against Phoenix was their most devastating offensive performance to date.

The Suns' game marked the homecoming of Connie Hawkins after nearly a decade of unfair exile by the NBA growing out of the college basketball fixes in 1961. Hawkins had
never thrown a game or shaved a point, nor had he been
asked to do so, nor had he asked anyone else to do so, but
J. Walter Kennedy (the Commissioner of the NBA) and
the powers-that-be had determined that he was not a character of NBA quality. Finally, Hawkins' impending lawsuit
and the cutthroat competition with the upstart ABA encouraged the established league to change its mind, so
Hawkins is in the big time.

He received a great ovation from the crowd, which did
not match the Laker or SuperSonic crowds for size or vol-
ume. In the early going, Hawkins was singularly unexciting,
and so was the ballgame. At certain times, like the last 5
minutes of the Laker game last Saturday, the thousands of
people at the Garden are as in one room, at one party, although most are hundreds of feet away across the court.
When the game is slow, however, and the crowd is quiet,
the feeling changes. Your immediate vicinity becomes a cu-
bicle and the voices of the people around you seem amplified
in relation to the people only a few feet farther away. It is
far more personal, but a less-rewarding experience. There
is something in the communal fervor that adds to the enjoyment of a basketball game or any sports event. Saturday
night it was there. On Tuesday night, until late in the game,
it was not.

The Knicks took a 30–25 lead at the end of a closely
played first quarter. Phoenix was pressing the Knicks, forcing them to use a large portion of the 24-second clock before they got close to the basket. Once the Knicks even
failed to beat the clock, and were forced into taking bad
shots on several other occasions. (I turned to the girl next
to me and explained to her what was happening, illustrating
by pointing out the bad shot Walt Frazier was, at that mo-

ment, being forced to take. Frazier, 20 feet from the basket and falling away, did not miss.)

Perhaps because he was so noticeable—or perhaps because of the quiet crowd—I noticed a gentleman behind me who wins the Most Obnoxious Fan of the Year award. (I know it is early in the season, but this guy will not be stopped.) It was not bad enough that he did a nonstop commentary on the ballgame and that his comments were couched in the most simplistic sportcasting jargon, he was also quite frequently all wrong. ("What a shot by Russell!" "Hey, where's May? How come he's not playing?" "He is? He hit a basket last time downcourt?")

In the second quarter the game got sloppier and the crowd sleepier, until Walt Frazier started to perform his magic and everything came to life. Frazier, almost on his own, commandeered the Knicks to a 62–49 halftime lead. Hawkins, to this point, had taken only three shots, and the Suns looked totally incapable of making a run at closing the deficit.

At halftime, for the first time this year basketball was not the primary topic of conversation within earshot. The Jets, the Mets, and the mayoralty race had been more exciting recently than the Knicks after that dull first half. The Knicks' big lead over a mediocre team that was playing at less than its potential had been accomplished despite sloppiness and stumbling. People settled in for the second half yawning, but the Knicks—sparked by Walt Frazier—soon woke them up.

With 6 minutes to go in the third quarter, Frazier saved the game from becoming a cliffhanger and sparked one of the most awesome and prolonged displays of offensive pyrotechnics that any fan could hope to see. Phoenix had fallen behind, 72–54, but a 3-point play by Phoenix had some sloppy Knick passing had contrived to cut the lead to 74–62. Again, Phoenix stopped the Knicks from scoring and worked the ball to Connie Hawkins. A basket here would have cut the margin to 10 points, with the momentum all with the visitors. Frazier turned the game around by stealing the ball from Hawkins and sparking a fast break that widened the margin to 76–62. From there the Knicks went on to a 97–78 third-quarter lead and a 140–116 victory.

The 43-point fourth quarter got everybody stirring, and it was not the usual guns doing the firing. Mike Riordan was the Frazier of the action—stealing the ball, setting up teammates for fast-break layups, wrapping the ball around his body on passes. Barnett and Stallworth shot well, but Russell was the man with an eye for the hoop. His shooting was uncanny as he piled up points on a bewildering variety of jumps, hooks, drives, and rebound shots. In the end everybody scored a bit, and everybody but the Suns went home happy.

If the Laker game illustrated the Knicks' ability to withstand pressure against a tough team, the Phoenix game illustrated the extent of their depth. It is currently outstanding and improving. Already, Russell substitutes only for Bradley and Stallworth only for DeBusschere. Riordan has developed into a fine, hustling defensive guard. Johnny Warren looked exceptionally good in his brief stint against Phoenix, and it may not be long before Barnett and Frazier each have their own caddy. Currently, Riordan would have to be considered the first sub, regardless of who needs a rest, but Warren has the potential to create the same happy situation at guard that already exists at forward.

The only potential trouble spot for the Knicks' bench is at center. Nate Bowman can shoot and jump and run, but he has bad hands. He can neither catch the ball nor hold onto it, so his other talents are somewhat wasted. "Hands" are something an athlete either has or does not, and the hope for Bowman to improve greatly must be considered slim. However, if Phil Jackson comes back in the winter, as hoped, he would provide top relief at both center and forward. Hosket is preferable to Bowman in certain situations —he is stronger—but Bill is really a forward. Donnie May suffers for being a Knickerbocker. He is a good ballplayer and would probably play lot at forward or guard with another team.

So the Knicks are 5–0. Tonight they face the Warriors, tomorrow night they will be in Detroit against the Pistons, and Saturday night they are at home again against the Bullets. Today a friend of mine said that if he fell asleep for six months and woke up to find the Knicks had gone 82–0 he would have been sorry he missed it, but not really surprised. They will not go 82–0, or even 80–2. But it is clear that the new age has arrived and that the 1969–70 Knickerbockers will be one of the great teams in modern sports.

OCTOBER 29

The Knickerbockers played about as badly as they can play on Thursday night. Willis Reed got only five rebounds, Cazzie Russell missed two technical foul shots, only Bill Bradley could hit from outside. They lost, deservedly, to a tough, well-coached San Francisco Warrior team, but by only 3 points. There are two reasons for the margin being so slender: the Knicks' tenacious defense and the fact that Nate Thurmond was ejected from the game halfway through the second quarter. In his brief stint, Thurmond had beaten Reed for 13 points.

And the Knicks managed to make even the loss interesting. They were down by 11 at the half but managed to spurt to within 1 point late in the third quarter. They again fell behind by 11 with 6 minutes to go in the game and again spurted to within a point. But neither time could they hit the basket to pull them ahead.

The crowd always expected them to. The reaction around me at the final buzzer, with the scoreboard reading 109–112 (left to right), was one of shock that the game had ended. That buzzer should have signaled a time-out, or the end of the third quarter. A basketball game just couldn't end with the Knickerbockers behind. Yet, after a five-game winning streak, it did. And, with Milwaukee and Philadelphia still undefeated at that time, the Knicks tumbled to third place.

But that sorry condition has been rectified. A television audience on Friday night saw the Knicks run away from a sloppy and uncoordinated Detroit team to end any thoughts that the single defeat was any more than that, a single defeat. I am sure I was not alone, but as I left the Garden after the Warrior game, I had the nagging fear that the fates were again to deprive the Knick fan of a championship team. It seemed impossible—Frazier and Reed were too good, Bradley and DeBusschere and Barnett too solid, the bench too deep, to allow that to happen. This team could *not* fall apart.

And Saturday night they showed the home fans, in person, that everything was still quite all right. The Baltimore Bullets, the generally acknowledged "team to beat" in the East for New York, were run off the floor. The final score was 128–99, and—as the cliché goes—it was not that close.

Frazier and Bradley were the big heroes that night, a pattern they seem to be establishing for the early going this season. "Dollar Bill" had the hot hand from outside, leading the scorers, and Frazier performed his ballhandling wizardry in making life thoroughly miserable for Earl Monroe, from whom he stole the ball twice.

Willis Reed picked up his third foul in the middle of the second quarter, but Nate Bowman came in and did a creditable job, for a change. When Bowman himself picked up four quick fouls (running his total to five) in the third quarter, Bill Hosket came in to play the pivot and finished the runaway there. Hosket played well against Wes Unseld, last year's top rookie and MVP, but a center who is only a short sequoia at 6-foot-8.

The crowd in New York does not leave early, partly because it recognizes that professional skills are on exhibition regardless of the score, and partially for a series of other interests it has built up. The fellow on my left, a middle-aged man who resembled a graying bulldog, revealed one of those interests with the first words he spoke as he took his seat.

"What are the points?"

This man did not even know me—though he had sat in that seat before—but he assumed that I would know the gambling spread. Madison Square Garden is full of people who know the spread, and bet the spread. In the new era, when the Knicks are heavy favorites most of the time, they are required to cover the spread—not just win the game—to send everybody home happy.

The second sudsidiary interest of the Knick fan is whether the Knicks can hold the opposition to under 100 points, something they manage to do more often than any other team in basketball. In this age of basketball, to do so is quite an accomplishment. To achieve this against an explosive offensive team like Baltimore is even more impressive. When Bob Quick of Baltimore shot two foul shots only seconds from the buzzer, the fans were very much concerned, despite the fact that the Knicks' 30-point lead beat even the most liberal point spread. Hitting them both would have given Baltimore the century. Quick, under a barrage of screaming pressure that must have astounded him, missed the first shot.

The Baltimore game dramatized Bill Bradley's emergence as a defensive forward. He gave Jack Marin fits. Marin is strong and fast, with a good outside shot, but he had trouble even getting the ball against Bradley. He just could not get open. There was some discussion going on around me that Bradley should be moved to guard. At one time it was clear that he could not handle it. He wasn't quick enough defensively, nor a good enough ballhandler. This may no longer be true, and if Phil Jackson comes back in December, giving the Knicks even more strength up front, maybe Holzman will consider the experiment. Barnett is playing well, but old legs can tire as the season wears on. Riordan is always adequate, sometimes excellent, but still inconsistent. Warren will be very good, but maybe not very soon. If Walt Frazier ever gets into foul trouble in a tight game, Bradley's versatility might be extremely useful.

Bill Hosket was quoted by Larry Merchant in Monday's *Post* on the fact that Knick fans do not leave early, a fact I mentioned earlier. "The crowds in New York want to see the young players do well. In other cities the crowds are leaving by the end of the game." That is true, and it is also true that if Bill Bradley becomes a part-time guard, the experiment will start at the end of a runaway. No self-respecting Knick fan would miss it.

The Knicks close out the first phase of this season with three home games this week. Richie Guerin leads his Atlanta Hawks in tonight, San Diego follows on Thursday, and Milwaukee on Saturday. After the meeting with Alcindor and his gang, the Knicks are gone for five games in ten days, which will comprise the next great test of their season. Currently at 7–1, with three home games coming up, they have started off fine. If they can continue a respectable pace through "roadwork," the NBA might as well start engraving the trophy.

A columnist said earlier this week that the only thing more boring than losing all the time was winning all the time. I don't agree. If Knick fans don't mind watching a runaway ballgame, I doubt that they'll object to a runaway season. All it takes to find out is to have one.

NOVEMBER 13

It has been two weeks since I put a word down for these pages, and the Knicks have played eight games since then. The story has been the same: Three times in the Garden and five times on the road, the Knicks have won. They beat Atlanta. They trounced San Diego at home, then came back two nights later to squeeze by Milwaukee, despite 36 points by Lew Alcindor. The road show visited Milwaukee, Phoenix, San Diego, Los Angeles, and San Francisco, and, despite Cazzie Russell's inability to play (bad back) for most of the trip, a broken nose suffered by Dave DeBusschere in Los Angeles, and Willis Reed's broken denture in the San Francisco game, the Knicks have extended a winning streak to ten games since the Warriors beat them in the Garden. They are now 15–1, one triumph away from the league's fastest start and their own mark for consecutive victories. They are also six full games ahead of the Eastern pack, five in the lost column. And the season is not yet one-fifth over.

As if this were not enough, the Knicks are still getting help from very strange places. Bill Bradley was tried at guard, first against San Diego two weeks ago when Frazier got into foul trouble, and several times since. He is showing that he can play there. Donnie May came off the bench in Phoenix when Russell was hurt to spark a rally that led to a big victory, and he had been the least illustrious of the twelve Knicks this year. Nate Bowman, who had earned little but laughs earlier, played great ball against Lew Alcindor in the home game against Milwaukee, which the Knicks won 112–108 despite losing Reed for a while to foul trouble. Riordan continues to be a frequent sensation, Stallworth has had brilliant moments.

There's talk that the Knickerbockers are one of the greatest teams of all time. Joe Lapchick, the venerable old ex-

Celtic and St. John's coach, says they are *the* best. Walt Frazier was quoted in the paper saying the loss to the Warriors took the pressure off the Knicks to achieve an 82–0 season. He was kidding, but some fans must be wondering how close they can come.

Most of the games have not been very close. The Knicks are winning the way the UCLA teams won before Lew Alcindor with periodic spurts of a couple minutes' duration that make runaways out of close games. In the game against San Diego at the Garden, which the Knicks won 123–110, the Knicks started the third quarter with 9 points in a row, the fourth quarter with 6. For the rest of the game, they played almost dead even.

Almost as often as not, the opposition fails to score 100 points and the local fans are extremely disappointed when they do. In the San Diego game, the Rockets hit the century mark with over 2 minutes to go and there was audible booing.

The talk of the league is the Knick defense, a masterful demonstration of teamwork created by Holzman. The "helping out" becomes so intense at times that it resembles a fifth-grade-team "swarm" for the ball, but it results in steals, rebounds, and a dramatic *esprit de corps*. Bill Bradley has become a master of playing between his man and the ball to the point that opposing forwards (even a Mel Counts, who carries over a half-foot height advantage) exhaust themselves attempting to get the ball.

After that extended road trip, the schedule now becomes more sane. The Knicks have three consecutive home games —against Chicago, Boston, and Cincinnati—before a road game at Philadelphia next Friday night. There will not be another long road trip until January, when they leave town for eight games in three weeks. Very shortly there will be little question that the Knicks can't be stopped for the Eastern Division, then attention will center around just how many games they can win.

Things have been shaken up around the league. Jerry Lucas was traded from Cincinnati to San Francisco for Jimmy King and Bill Turner. Not more than a week after the trade, King was injured and is shelved indefinitely. That is not the only problem the Royals have; Bob Cousy has been trying to get a playing release from Boston, his old team, so that he can play for the Royals, but Boston GM Red Auerbach is making the deal impossible. Auerbach has troubles of his own. Without Bill Russell, the Boston dynasty has crumbled to a 3–9 record and a firm grip on the cellar. Even Celtic pride can do little without the Bearded Wonder.

Los Angeles, which was not winning in big bunches anyway, lost Wilt Chamberlain—probably for the season—to a ripped knee tendon. The load now returns to Baylor and West, but they are older now and don't have a good picking and passing center like Darrall Imhoff to make things easier anymore. Joe Mullaney, the new Laker coach, insists that the team can come back, but they are 5–6 now and trailing 11–3 Atlanta (which doesn't seem to miss Zelmo Beatty much at all) by a considerable margin for this early in the season. Those preseason prognostications may not look too good very shortly.

I will redouble my efforts to speak to players and officials of opposing teams, beginning with Chick Hearn, the Los Angeles Laker broadcaster whom I am scheduled to see on the Lakers' next trip in. Letters to the publicists for all the NBA teams have borne no fruit so far.

My editor argued with me that the Knicks had to lose some ballgames to make an interesting book. He feels that a runaway season will lack drama and character. I strongly disagree. The Knicks may prove this year to be what has never been before in sport—a charismatic juggernaut. Unlike the Mets, who won a championship with a believable record, the Knicks are on their way to an incredible season. As the number of wins increases and the record percentage is maintained (it is currently .938), there will be a different kind of drama generated and a different tenor completely from anything that has previously existed in professional sports. The creation of perfection, or its close cousins, is always exciting, and the Knicks' season may fall into that category. Perhaps 20 percent of a season is not a big enough sample on which to base conclusions, but a 15–1 record is terribly convincing. So are the Knicks.

NOVEMBER 16

The bulldog-looking fellow on my left has told me quite a bit about the gambling that takes place on the basketball games, and one of the tips he offered was never to bet a point spread in double figures. Last night he broke his own rule, giving 12 points to take the Knicks over the Bill Russell-less Celtics, and won $500. Holding the opposition under 100 points for the ninth time this season (in eighteen starts), the Knicks won 113–98. They have now won twelve straight games, a club record, and have started the season with a mark of 17–1, a league record. A friend of mine in Los Angeles called this morning and remarked that the Knicks were doing well. I told him, jokingly, that they might not lose again. He said he figures they must lose at least once more.

Between the victory over Chicago on Thursday night and last night's win over the Celtics, I was in Washington to participate in the anti-war protest on Friday night and Saturday. On Thursday night I remarked to the fellow on my right that I was flying down. He was unaware that a March was taking place. I wondered whether his ignorance of this political protest, which has been on the front page of every newspaper for a week, was indicative of a general ignorance among Knick fans. Indeed, he seems like a reasonably intelligent, well-informed, college-educated gentleman. It must make you wonder.

The Knicks started sloppily against Chicago on Thursday night, allowing a 30–22 first-quarter deficit to expand to 34–24 before the inevitable explosion. Then, sparked by Dave Stallworth and Walt Frazier, the Knicks went on a tear that gave them a 53–48 halftime advantage—including 10 quick points that knotted the game at 34. Willis Reed had a picnic with Tom Boerwinkle, the Bulls' center. Boerwinkle is tall and a good shooter, but much too slow to stay with the nimble Willis. The Knick center and captain led the scorers, as he has regularly since the beginning of the last road trip, with 27 points.

The Knicks' 10-point explosion in the second quarter woke up a sleeping crowd and, for a brief time, the spirit of jubliant community reached its season peak. After the middle of the third quarter, however, the Knicks clearly had the game salted away and the only questions were whether they could beat the point spread of 10½ and hold the Bulls under 100 points. With a steal and a basket by Frazier in the final 10 seconds, they did both.

Being at last night's game against the Celtics was a peculiar experience. I had been trapped with several friends in the tear-gas barrage that the police in Washington fired at some of the more violent protesters on Friday night. None of us caught a direct hit, but the apartment house lobby in which we took refuge entertained a stream of young people over a two-hour period who were retreating with serious discomfort. The experience of assisting these people, many of them scared and all of them angered, was strangely incongruous with the jubilant, clean-shaven company in which I found myself on Saturday night at Madison Square Garden.

The once-proud Celtics came to town with a 3–11 record, hopeful that rookie Jo-Jo White, just released from six months in Marine Reserve Training, could help reverse the downward spiral that the retirements of Bill Russell and Sam Jones had engendered. Henry Finkel, late of the Lakers and Rockets—and second-string for both—was the Celtics' starting center. At times the backcourt, which was once the domain of Cousy and Sharman, Jones and Jones, was manned by Don Chaney and White. The New York crowd, for the most part, felt no sympathy for the fallen champs. They were anxious to see the Knicks deliver the final blow to the Celtic dynasty; they had felt personally shackled by it for over a decade. Led by Reed, again with 27 points, and the best game Dave DeBusschere has played at home this year, the locals did not disappoint their fans. Walt Frazier sparked a spree in the first quarter that created a 34–20 advantage at the end of the stanza. A brief Celtic flurry before halftime cut the margin at the break to 54–46, but the Knicks came out running in the third quarter and ended any doubts. The outcome of the game was so clearly determined by the middle of the fourth quarter that John Havlicek, the Celtics' tireless captain and last remaining superstar, was taken out. Incidentally, Henry Finkel led the Celtic scoring with 20 points.

DeBusschere was a marvel. Dave broke his nose a week ago in Los Angeles and is playing with a protective piece over it, taped on conspicuously across the forehead and the cheeks. The narrow slit through which he must view the action seems not to impair his vision, but the whole assembly must serve as a painful reminder of what can happen under the boards. He is not intimidated. He has been playing his helpful style of ball all season, setting picks, crashing the boards, playing solid defense, and scoring when it is needed the most. Frazier and Bradley have gotten most of the raves, Reed has been the dominant force for the last two weeks, and Barnett has gone on the scoring flurries of which only he is capable. But DeBusschere's workmanlike play has gone largely unnoticed except by the more sophisticated Knick fans. Even Dave Stallworth, DeBusschere's substitute, has upstaged him frequently with his aggressive defensive play, flashy drives, and long-range jump-shooting. Last night, however, DeBusschere scored 18 points as well as playing a superb all-around game, and it was recognized by everyone.

My gambling friend and I had a long talk at halftime on Thursday night, and it covered much more than basketball. There are teeth missing from his grin; his square face and short, stocky stature is truly reminiscent of a bulldog; but he is, as he pointed out to me, "no dummy." What we discussed, whether society should impose moral judgments through legislation, is tangential to the point. His thoughtfulness about subjects totally unrelated to basketball is the point. I hope that he is not unique among Knick fans.

NOVEMBER 22

After the Knicks trounced Cincinnati on Tuesday, 112–94, not playing nearly as well as they can, I was beginning to wonder whether the game pattern they seemed to have established would ever be broken. After opening up a slight lead in the first quarter, the Knicks spurt in the second period. Slowing down slightly, they usually relinquish some of the lead they had built up and retire at halftime with a narrower margin. Then a well-rested first-string (the bench having played for a good part of the second quarter) puts away the game by the end of the third period, with the final 12 minutes of the game left for beating the point spread, holding the opposition under 100 points, and exercise for the "scrubeenies," and meditation.

The Cincinnati game followed form beautifully, with the only real deviation being that Dave DeBusschere was one of the offensive bulwarks and Walt Frazier's shooting continued to slump. A lively capacity crowd cheered the Knicks quickly off the mark, and New York grabbed a 12–3 lead

31

in the first 4 minutes. The Royals, however, having read the script and knowing it wasn't time yet to be put away, battled back to within a basket at times, and trailed 27–20 at the end of the quarter.

The rarest of occurrences, a series of turnovers by Walt Frazier, kept the Royals close throughout the second quarter, and the Knick lead was down to 50–45 at halftime. Six minutes into the third quarter, however, the lead was expanded to 65–52, and at the end of the period it stood at 80–68. A hot fourth quarter by Cazzie Russell maintained the broad margin for a victory, a point-spread victory, and a successful (i.e., under 100 points) defensive effort.

Bob Cousy is coaching at Cincinnati this season, and on the afternoon preceding the Knick game finally dealt for his playing release from the Celtics. Cooz did not suit up for the game at the Garden, however, much to the disappointment of the fans, who gave him a fine ovation during the pregame introductions.

Oscar Robertson was also loudly applauded when he was introduced, but his Royal teammates did not show the same deference to him that the fans did—nor that his teammates had in years past. Norm Van Lier and Herm Gilliam, rookie guards, handled the ball far more than Royal guards alongside the Big O had in the past, with the result that Robertson got only 2 assists and 18 points. A peek at the league scoring statistics, which list Oscar at 24.3 points per game and averaging 7.3 assists, indicates that what happened in New York does not happen every night. However, the trading of Jerry Lucas suggests that Bob Cousy recognizes no sacred cows in Ohio and is determined to install old-time Celtic-style basketball at any price, even—temporarily—losing. An offense that is dominated by one player will not fit Cousy's mold.

The New York Knickerbocker Team Victory Pattern was disrupted seriously last night in a televised game from Philadelphia. I made a point of watching the game because I suspected that the 76ers would be big trouble, despite a 6–11 record coming in and, statistically, the worse defensive performance in the league (125 point-per-game yield). Even without Luke Jackson, who is in uniform but still resting a tender knee, I couldn't believe that Philadelphia was that bad. Hal Greer is still a great guard and he has able companionship in the backcourt with Wally Jones and Archie Clark. Billy Cunningham is a stellar All-Star at forward, and his running mate, Jim Washington, is capable, though not outstanding. Darrall Imhoff is one of the unappreciated centers in the game. He isn't strong like Reed or Thurmond, but he is a smart ballplayer who helps his teammates get open and can pass well.

Nonetheless, the Knicks started in standard fashion. A close first quarter gave way to a Knick spurt and an 18-point lead, whittled down to 8 by the 76ers by halftime. The Knicks, who will soon run out of streak records to pursue, were after their fourteenth-straight victory, ninth-straight on the road, nineteen out of twenty to start the season. When the lead expanded to 12 points in the third quarter, it looked like the 76ers, playing New York for the first time this season, had learned their roles quickly.

But they had not. Led by Cunningham, Philadelphia fought back and pulled to within a basket at 94–92 and 96–94. In the final 15 seconds there was the constant flurry of times-out, fouls, and pressing, which mark the conclusion of close basketball games (but which have been absent from Knickerbocker games this year). Walt Frazier helped keep matters close by missing four foul shots out of six attempted in the last half-minute. The second series of missed shots resulted in Philadelphia getting a crack at tying the game with 5 seconds left. However, Greer fumbled a jump-shot attempt while under severe pressure from Barnett and Bradley, and Willis Reed recovered the ball. Reed then sank two free throws with one second to go to supply the final margin, 98–94.

The Knicks, in general, have not been playing as explosively during the past couple of weeks as they did earlier in the season. Frazier, particularly, is lapsing on offense. The superior strength, speed, depth, and defensive ability of the team has carried them anyhow and, until last night, has kept them from being severely threatened. However, a rigorous schedule this week, with home games against Phoenix, Los Angeles, and Detroit, and road games against Atlanta and Cincinnati—all in eight days—will test the club severely unless the groove is found again.

Very quickly, the Knickerbockers have established a standard for themselves where merely winning a lot of games and finishing first in the division would fall short of expectations. The accolade "best basketball team ever assembled" has been showered from many sides, so they are expected to win, win, win. Bill Bradley commented that winning explosively and decisively, as they have, is fun. Despite the fact that they have consistently covered the point spread (sixteen out of twenty times this year), Bradley denied that the spread entered the players' minds. Winning is fun, playing well is fun. The joy, for the players and the fans this year, lies in the skillful and often awesome execution of which the Knicks are capable. It is this that is reflected in the final score. They are supposed to win—that is expected.

NOVEMBER 25

Chick Hearn, the Los Angeles Laker announcer who also carries the title "Director of Communications," replied to my request to the Laker publicist for an interview. Calling Hearn at the Statler Hilton last night, however, as per my instructions, I found him too busy to chat this time around,

34

but he promised fairly cheerfully to do so in Los Angeles in January, when I will be out there to record.

It may be just as well that Hearn couldn't be interviewed now, because the problems of the Lakers must be weighing heavily on his professional basketball mind. The defending Western Division champs were supposed to be the super-team, sporting Chamberlain, Baylor, and West for the second year in a row. This season, without the scourge of Bill Russell to block their path, they hoped to bring the first professional basketball championship to Los Angeles.

But injuries have struck hard. Chamberlain ruptured a tendon in his knee and will not be back until late winter, if at all this season. Baylor has been sidelined with a groin injury. Indeed, the Lakers are down to six fairly healthy players, and West is playing with a slight muscle pull. Despite all this, they had won four in a row before losing badly to Baltimore on Sunday night.

The Knicks, on the other hand, seemed to pull themselves together offensively on Saturday night against Phoenix. Willis Reed scored 37 points and Dave DeBusschere 25 in leading New York to a convincing twentieth victory of the season. Most amazing about the game, perhaps, was that Dick Barnett handed off twelve assists, his career mark.

The Suns are going to be a very strong team by the end of this season. Jerry Chambers, as I predicted before the season started, has been inserted in the starting lineup and is scoring. His outside-shooting ability creates more room for Connie Hawkins and Dick Van Arsdale to drive, and it is ultimately on the ability of these two men to operate offensively that the Suns' fortunes rest. Neal Walk has replaced Jim Fox as the starting center for Phoenix and is showing less intimidation about using his bulk than in his first Garden appearance. Walk will do better against other centers than against Willis Reed, who is equally strong and far more experienced and agile. Gail Goodrich is a better ballplayer without the pressure of an entire offense resting on him. Paul Silas is a better forward than most teams can afford to bring off the bench, as Phoenix does.

There was some question, when the idea for this book was originally submitted, about how the chapters would break down. The standard procedure is to submit a book with a chapter outline and a one- or two-chapter sample of text. Hardly being a seer of what was to occur with the Knicks, I suggested that the ups-and-downs of the Knicks would create natural chapter breaks in the book. But obviously that will not work—unless the Knicks do a disastrous about-face. The real breakdown so far cannot be shown precisely but rather by a trend. At the beginning of the year, Walt Frazier and Bill Bradley spearheaded the Knickerbocker victories. They are still vital—Frazier to move the ball and Bradley to generate movement without the ball. The crucial leadership, however, has fallen upon Willis Reed and Dave DeBusschere. These are the men who have, over the last ten games, supplied the key basket, the key rebound, the key blocked shot. DeBusschere's play has been breathtaking. His aggressiveness on defense and under both boards has never been questioned, but his recent efforts have been almost superhuman. Though at 13.8 he still has the lowest scoring average among the Knick starters, he has been shooting the eyes out of the basket lately, and from distances that Barnett and Bradley do not attempt.

Reed is the unquestioned team leader. He is the leading scorer (23.9 to date) and the leading rebounder. He consistently does a strong job on the opposing center, whether it be Lew Alcindor or Jim Fox. His mobility on the outside, setting screens, and maneuvering for jump shots and drives inspire disbelief that he is really 6-foot-10 and 235, as the program lists.

The Knicks are currently in pursuit of the league record for consecutive wins, which was set at seventeen by Washington (1946) and Boston (1959). Assuming they can polish off the injury-riddled Lakers tonight (who, we must remember, still have Jerry West in the lineup), they will seek to tie the record at Atlanta tomorrow and break it at Cleveland against Cincinnati on Friday night.

And with this magnificent beginning, it is interesting to note that they must keep up the pace almost as well as they've set it to match the 1966–67 Philadelphia 76ers, the Wilt Chamberlain-led team that beat Boston. The 76ers were 26–2, 36–3, and 45–4 on their way to a 68–13 season's record. The Knicks are currently 20–1.

Attendance on Saturday night fell just short of capacity, and the Knicks, averaging roughly 16,000 per game, are running way ahead of their league attendance mark, set last season. One of the fans around me was discussing friends of his who had decided not to get season tickets "this year," since they would have been ordering them late and unable to get seats very close to the floor. The fellow who was relating the story indicated his feeling that Knick tickets will soon be (for 41 games) as difficult to get as season football tickets (for 7 games). If this is true, the ongoing right to purchase tickets for the following season may become very valuable.

Because of the number of season subscribers, there is a great continuity of the fans' reaction to the game. The affectionate reaction to Nate Bowman's antics, which have been secondary to the yeoman job he has been doing as back-up center of late, are a product of accumulated knowledge that all the fans share. Leftovers from last year—among whom I do not number, having been in Los Angeles—appreciate the development of Mike Riordan from scrub to solid performer and look for signs of the same from Johnny Warren. Dave Stallworth is improving with every game, a fact that would not be appreciated nearly so much by fans who did not appear regularly.

37

Recent quotes in the paper, particularly from Bill Bradley, indicate that fan reactions help set a psychological mood for the Knicks and, once they catch fire, keeps them burning. At this pace it will be difficult to tell just how much home fans do help. There isn't much to choose between a 9–0 road record and an 11–1 home mark. This is the standard barometer to determine home-court advantage. It may be necessary to look at the difference in average winning margin to glean evidence that the fans are helping. Incidentally, the Knick average winning margin, roughly 15 points, is about 10 points higher than that of the NBA team that stands second.

NOVEMBER 29

In Cleveland last night against the Cincinnati Royals, the Knickerbockers rallied for 6 points in the last 16 seconds to win their eighteenth-straight game, a new professional record. Walt Frazier, whose problems at the foul line nearly resulted in defeat against Philadelphia last Friday night, hit two free throws with 2 seconds left to put the locals over the top.

The record is not the only Knickerbocker news this week. The ballgames against Los Angeles on Tuesday at the Garden and at Atlanta on Wednesday were stories in themselves. The decimated Lakers tried a strange ploy against the Knicks, sending four players to a sideline and isolating Jerry West against a frustrated single defender on the other side. The NBA rule against a zone defense, combined with the strengthening rule against defensive players remaining in the foul lane when they are not guarding their man, resulted in the Knicks' drawing two technical fouls in the first half in attempting to assist the unfortunate Dick Barnett, Mike Riordan, or Walt Frazier in guarding West. In the second half, a double-team was attempted, but this created a 4-on-3 mismatch on the other side of the court, and the sharp-passing West gave his teammates some easy shots. Jerry shot 15-for-24 from the floor and totaled 41 points, but the Knicks managed to win by a half-dozen anyhow. The strategy by Laker coach Mullaney was brilliant, even if ultimately unsuccessful, and may lead to a re-evaluation of the league's ban on zone defenses. The Knicks, on the other hand, showed that teamwork ultimately wins ballgames, even against as great an adversary as West.

The point was driven home more firmly in the seventeenth-consecutive victory at Atlanta on Wednesday night. A monster third quarter, during which the Knicks outscored the Hawks 32–5 at one stretch, paced a 138–108 victory over a strong, winning team that had been playing well. The reviews of the Knick performance were unanimous: It was the best exhibition of basketball for one quarter in the memory of any living observer of the game. Richie Guerin went further, stating that Walt Frazier gave the best individual performance—during those 12 minutes—that he had ever seen.

The devastation was so total as to be incredible. Reed scored 16 points and Frazier 12 while Atlanta scored 12 in the period. Only three times in the twelve minutes were the Hawks able to penetrate for a shot close to the basket, and the Knicks stole the ball time and time again. Bill Bradley and Frazier were the primary thieves, removing the ball from Atlanta's possession as simply as they remove it from the rack for shooting practice before a game. The effortlessness of the demonstration made it even more frightening— even for Knick fans it was a bit frightening. Perfection, in its beauty, is always a little intimidating, and the Knick performance was as close to perfection as rapid-fire basketball action will allow. Frazier and Reed finally wound up with 33 points apiece while contributing to Richie Guerin's "most embarrassing quarter" in fifteen years of professional ball.

We Knick fans might have believed, after Wednesday, that the magic that ran opponents off the floor at the beginning of the season had been retrieved from its mysterious hiding place. The Knicks during the winning streak have often been less impressive than they were in the mini-streak of five games that began the season. Again, against Cincinnati, they had to be pushed near the brink before recovering for victory.

It is clear—and surely even the staunchest professional basketball fan would not deny—that baseball and football attract more attention from the public and press than basketball does. This is true for a combination of reasons, none of which indicate that the situation will change in the near future. Therefore it is particularly noteworthy that the Knicks are drawing the increased attention of the New York sports pages, even as football remains big news. The *Daily News* is beginning a series by Phil Pepe on the Knicks this week; *The New York Times* has changed its professional basketball box score for the Knicks to include such esoteric statistics as minutes played, rebounds, and assists in addition to points by each player. The glory is shared somewhat with the New York Rangers, who occupy first place in the National Hockey League East and have been playing exclusively nonlosing hockey for a couple of weeks now themselves. But the Knicks' devastation of the pro ranks is the primary sports news and, increasingly, the talk of the town.

For all the communciation that we have among the people in the section, the only name I know is of the fellow on my right, Dan. There is a lack of personal friendship among the people who often sit together twice a week at the Garden. Names are not automatically exchanged. This does not indicate that people do not become friendly—they do, and inquiries about insensitive personal matters (such as health) occur smoothly and habitually. I think there is a certain amount of frustration on the part of some people that they don't get to know their neighbors better, but the season is still young and those frustrations may evolve into friendships before the last playoff game is played.

At least two organizations of Knick fans, the "2-Pointer Club" and the "Knickerbocker Bench-Warmers' Club," have sent me requests to join, having used the season-subscribers' mailing list. The latter club seems interesting, it being a succession of eight luncheons that Knick players attend. The flyer promises that you will develop a "first-name relationship" with the Knick players and that you will have the opportunity to ask them "any questions you like." That is not quite $200 worth of interesting.

Tonight the Detroit Pistons come in for the first time this year, which leaves Philadelphia as the only club that hasn't appeared. The Knicks beat the Pistons in the seventh game of the year, bouncing back from their lone defeat to run Van Breda Kolff's charges silly in Detroit. The Pistons are a strange team. With Walker, Bing, Miles, Bellamy, and Dischinger backed by Komives, Moore, and other strong reserves, one would think they'd be a winner. They just traded Happy Hairston to Los Angeles for Bill Hewitt, a second-year player with a lot of promise. Hairston was not getting along well with Van Breda Kolff, which is the apparent reason for the trade, since Hairston is an established pro, strong at both ends, and not old enough to be unloaded because of age. With playing time, Hewitt could develop, but what the Pistons really need is cohesiveness, a problem set back by turnovers in personnel. Their 7–13 record does not hold a torch to the Knicks' 23–1, but any team with as many good shooters as Detroit has can be tough on any given night. (And a cliché becomes a cliché because it is so true.)

DECEMBER 2

The first snow of the season fell on New York yesterday. It came in blustery, uncomfortable flurries, mixed with a cold rain that penetrated the best umbrellas and London Fog trenchcoats. This morning there was nothing left.

Perhaps the Knick game on Saturday night was an omen. Their play came in flurries against Detroit, and always with the uncomfortable notion that the normal Knickerbocker blitz would not materialize. When the game ended, the Knicks had lost for the second time this season and the powdery white cover of an eighteen-game winning streak had disappeared.

The Pistons played well and Van Breda Kolff coached smartly. Relying on the outside-shooting ability of Eddie Miles, Jimmy Walker, and Howard Komives, he spread his three guards wide, making it impossible for Frazier, Bradley, and Barnett to help each other out in the fashion by which they create their patented steals. All three of Detroit's guns were firing accurately, and they received considerable assistance with good rebounding by Otto Moore, who has replaced Walt Bellamy as Detroit's first-string center. The Knicks, for their part, were totally disoriented. Willis Reed and Frazier kept them in the game as the lead switched back and forth for three periods. But both did their job the hard way offensively, canning shots from greater distances than they normally attempt. Barnett and the subs, Russell, Riordan, and Stallworth, couldn't hit a thing.

When the Knicks lost to San Francisco a little over a month ago, there was the constant feeling that the explosion was moments away. In that game the Knicks kept fighting back, but just could not quite marshal the rally that would give them a lead. When the final buzzer sounded, the Knicks were in the midst of another rally and the lead had been cut to 3 points. They did not lose, so to speak. They ran out of time.

Such was not the case against Detroit. The Knicks carried a slim lead into the fourth quarter, but a pair of 3-point plays by Komives keyed a Detroit surge that carried them to a 110–98 victory going away. The deficit grew throughout the closing quarter as the Knicks showed frequent signs of mental, physical, and emotional fatigue. Willis Reed, par-

42

ticularly, was not himself. He fumbled passes and rebounds, blew layups, and just couldn't get himself off the ground on a crucial jump ball.

The fans were extremely disappointed at the loss, but equally graceful. The Knickerbockers received a five-minute standing ovation just prior to the individual introductions. This was for the winning streak—the record-breaking winning streak—which climaxed so magnificently on the road. First came the record-tying seventeenth victory at Atlanta, complete with a Devastating Third Quarter, then the Magnificent Comeback for the eighteenth triumph against the Royals. Both road games had been televised back to New York and the fans had seen and appreciated these victories, and suffered the frustration of not being able to have their heroes know it. The standing ovation let them know.

The applause for the Knicks started again, however, about two hours later while the last 30 seconds of the season's second defeat were ticking off. Any hope of victory had vanished as the Pistons extended their substantial lead. All the fans left in the Garden, no fewer than 99 percent of the capacity crowd that was there at the beginning, applauded.

So the magnificent streak has ended and the Knicks will try to start building another one against the Seattle Supersonics tonight. At the end of the week the Knicks have to encounter the Baltimore Bullets at Baltimore on Friday and Milwaukee at the Garden on Saturday. If another streak is about to begin, it will not come easy. The Bullets just had a nine-game winning streak of their own snapped by the Boston Celtics on Saturday night.

DECEMBER 9

The new winning streak is up to three. The front cover of *Newsweek* (out today) features Willis Reed scoring on a hook shot over Walt Bellamy (perhaps photographed during loss number 2 ten days ago). A win over Cincinnatti tonight would top Philadelphia's 26–2 start of 1966–67.

Last week's three victories were quite convincing. Seattle, the first opponent after the loss to Detroit, fell easily. If there was any team-morale problem engendered by a single defeat (should there *ever* be?), Seattle simply did not have the manpower to capitalize.

Friday night's game at Baltimore was televised, with a bonus replay of the frantic last 16 seconds of the Cincinnati game. The Baltimore game could almost be viewed as a microcosm of the Bullets' troubles for the season. For most of the game they matched New York, brilliant play for brilliant play, outside shot for outside shot, but a few brief New York flurries were sufficient to down the Bullets convincingly.

Saturday night the Knicks came back home to face Milwaukee and Lew Alcindor again. The last time the Bucks were in the Garden, the big streak was four games old and the game ended terrifyingly close, 112–108. This time, with a baby streak of two games to protect, the Knicks quickly left no doubt. It was 8–0 when Costello first called time out, and 10–0 before Lew got Milwaukee on the board. But 26 points and ten rebounds from the big rookie couldn't keep pace with Bill Bradley and the Knicks' balanced attack and fancy defense and feeding. "Dollar Bill" scored 29 points, grabbed six rebounds, and had five assists in 33 minutes in leading a 124–99 rout.

There are many in the press who consider the Knicks' performance on Saturday night their outstanding effort of the season. I was not impressed that way immediately but, in retrospect, must admit that it ranks near the top. It was a game of sustained brilliance, unlike the wild quarter-long flurries against Atlanta two weeks ago or against Seattle last Tuesday. At no time did the Knicks make the Bucks look like high school kids, as they had the Hawks and Sonics. However, at no time did the Knicks play anything but superlative ball, at no time were they threatened, and at no time were they not in absolute control of the game.

It is difficult to glean what the nation's reaction to the Knicks might be when you are in New York. The press here is impressed and Knick stories, biographies, interviews, and analyses abound. An article in *Sports Illustrated* last week hinted at the national interest; the *Newsweek* piece (four full pages long and entitled "The Dazzling Knicks") makes it quite clear that New York is not alone in marveling at the hardwood wonders. *Newsweek* indicated that the Knickerbockers could be a primary force (with Lew Alcindor and a host of potential superstars coming out of college ranks) in elevating professional basketball to new plateaus of popularity. They went as far as to suggest that their dynasty would endure the decade to come, a thought that had not entered the mind of too many Knick fans. After all, a 26–2 beginning and the prospect of a world championship was enough to savor after so many years of futility.

If the Knicks are a threat to stay this good for a long period of time, one must wonder whether fan interest *can* be sustained. I remember how hard it was to get a student ticket for UCLA games during Lew Alcindor's freshman year with an exciting frosh team and a competitive but not overwhelming varsity led by Edgar Lacey and Mike Lynn. In Lew's first varsity year, the problem—if anything—increased, with 13,000-seat Pauley Pavilion packed to the rafters every time the Bruins were home. By the second Alcindor year, however, some of the gloss had worn off. Interest centered on particular games when a challenge might be offered —against Houston, of course, and in the NCAA championship rounds—but it wasn't hard to find a ticket for the average home game. Surely, Pauley Pavilion continued to be nearly sold out, but there were increasing pockets of empty seats.

This is less likely to happen in New York with the Knicks, but it is conceivable. First of all, New York crowds are more sophisticated than L.A. crowds, particularly more sophisticated than L.A. college-basketball fans. The appreciation for the *way* the game is played quite frequently transcends the final score. (Else why would the Knicks have drawn so well when they were losers?) Secondly, the consummate skill of every player in the NBA makes it at least possible that (to repeat) any team can beat any other team on any given night (as Detroit proved ten days ago). It was inconceivable that the weaker college teams could give UCLA any kind of run for the money at all during the Alcindor era.

Tonight will be the New York fans' first chance to see Bob Cousy back in sneakers again with the Royals. Cooz threw the ball away on the crucial play in the Knicks' rally for their eighteenth straight ten days ago. He hasn't been playing much, but I just hope there's enough of the showman left in him to try it for a while tonight. The Royals come into the game at 11–16, tied for fifth place in the East, and the Knicks are 3-for-3 against them. However, none of the Royal games have been runaways, and Mr. Cousy's youngsters have certainly not seen the Knickerbockers at their best. It seems unlikely, at least superficially, that there is anything inherent in the Royals' material or style that should give the Knicks the trouble that they've had. Maybe tonight they'll make a true believer out of Cousy too. Maybe, if he's read *Newsweek*, they won't have to.

DECEMBER 11

When you start going to every Knick game after years of having been a less affluent and less regular attendee, the romance of going to the Garden diminishes to an extent. I had become fairly fixed in my habit of going into the Garden at Thirty-first Street and Eighth Avenue, bypassing the front lobby and getting to my seat in Section 111 by the quickest possible route. Unlike fans who are even older and more experienced, having been to every game for years, I usually still arrive early enough to watch layup drills. But seldom do I arrive in the lobby early anymore, as I did when I was younger, savoring the "ticket to the game" for its entire worth. A lot goes on in the Madison Square Garden lobby, as I found on Tuesday night when I revisited it for the first time in several weeks.

The game against Cincinnati was not a sellout, perhaps surprising in that Bob Cousy is back in uniform, the Royals had battled the Knicks tough in their first three meetings, and, most importantly, this game was the first meeting of the two teams since the "last-16-seconds" game in Cleveland. Even with "tickets available for tonight's game at windows 13 through 16," fans were hawking better seats to less fortunate brethren outside the Garden as well as on the ticket lines. I approached a fellow who had just bought a pair from an un-uniformed salesman and he told me he hadn't paid any premium—did I think he was crazy? The tickets he purchased were good ones, $7 seats, and the vendor probably had more company tickets for the night's game than he was going to use. Every one he disposed of put that much extra cash in his pocket.

At the center of the lobby, not 25 feet from the ticket windows, is a large-scale model of the Garden with a plastic dome surrounding it. The model looks like what I *thought* the Astrodome would be when they hadn't built it yet. The periphery of the model was lined two deep with fans craning their necks to see where the tickets they had purchased placed them, most of them having purchased tickets for the game about to begin in less than an hour. I wondered why they just didn't go inside. One fellow asked me where the best seats would be for the Ice Follies, inviting a few snickers from other people around us who recognized no legitimate entertainment for the Garden except basketball, hockey, and boxing. I told him I didn't know.

Still more than half-an-hour before gametime the public address system in the lobby sounded a warning about "unauthorized persons outside" who were selling tickets to *past* games. These tickets, obviously, were invalid.

I got inside early and wandered over to talk to Eddie Layton, the Garden organist. I've been feeling sorry for Layton since the season began, and I noticed that his organ is positioned so that his back is to the court while he's playing. I couldn't believe that the Knick brass could be so callous as to deliberately face him away, nor so stupid as to do it accidentally. Layton told me that the height of his organ dictated the positioning. He wouldn't be able to see over the top of it if it were positioned between him and the court. I wondered why they didn't place it sideways, but I didn't get an answer I could understand. However, he thought he might be getting a newer, smaller organ "soon."

Eddie Layton is very visible and very popular. As is the current vogue in professional sports, the organist serves to cheerlead the home crowd, not just to entertain during lulls in the game. Layton does his job very well, although he does not have the imagination of some other organists who try to play songs whose lyrics apply to the situation of the event. (The master of this is the organist for the California Angels, who plays the appropriate tune for each player as he comes to bat.) Layton's visibility encourages about 200 fans a night to come talk to him, by his estimate. He has been at the Garden for only a year and feels that the only change in Knick fans is that they have become slightly more enthusiastic this year over their winner.

Which brings us to the game against Cincinnati on Tuesday night, the third loss of the season. It was a heartbreaker.

Despite their depth, which should keep everybody well

rested, and Holzman's policy of playing everybody, which should keep everybody from getting rusty, the Knicks have been playing somewhat sluggish ball for a couple of weeks. DeBusschere and Bradley have played consistently well, but Frazier and Reed have not. Barnett has not been hitting the key shots, but his general play has not really been lacking. The bench has not really performed, with stirring exceptions the way it did earlier in the season. The primary puzzles, however, are Frazier and Reed.

Walt's problem has been partly of the making of opposition strategy. Starting with Bill van Breda Kolff in the game that Detroit won to snap the eighteen-game streak, the man Frazier guards has consistently been assigned to move away from the ball and away from the flow of play. This makes it extremely difficult for Frazier to double-team and get back to his man. Generally, the Knicks have played Barnett and Riordan on the opposition's top threat in the backcourt, on the theory that Frazier can handle the weaker of the two guards without his full attention and thus be free to help out. The Van Breda Kolff—spawned strategy may force the Knicks to play Frazier on the top guard so that a team that wants to take Walt out of the action hurts itself as badly as they hurt the Knicks. In either case, it is doubtful that Frazier will be able to steal the ball with the reckless abandon that he did earlier in the year when Holzman was a step ahead of everybody else.

Reed's problem may be something physical. The paper today mentions a sore toe—maybe that's it. In any case, Willis is not moving with the grace that Knick fans remember, neither on offense or defense. Against Cincinnati, this was extremely costly. Connie Dierking, a good center but no Reed, played 48 minutes and scored as many points (19) as Reed. Reed should have been able to take Dierking apart, particularly in the second half, when Willis, having been spelled by Bowman in the second quarter, was better rested than his counterpart. Willis should be too fast and too strong for Dierking. On Tuesday night he was not.

In addition, Willis missed the jump shot at the buzzer that would have tied the game for the Knicks, who fell 103–101. That was not the only problem, however, just the last one. The Knicks led, 101–98, but turnovers by Riordan, Reed, and DeBusschere ultimately lost the game, despite two missed foul shots by Royals' rookie Norm Van Lier that made Reed's last-ditch attempt possible.

The vital difference in the game, however, and the reason that the Royals give the Knickerbockers trouble, is Oscar Robertson. The Big O can control the tempo of a ballgame, simply because it is impossible to steal the ball from him. When he is permitted to control the game, the Royals rarely give up the ball without a good shot at the basket, which nullifies the Knickerbockers' primary source of victory, demoralizing fast breaks after stolen passes and forced turn-overs.

Johnny Green, erstwhile Knickerbocker stalwart and climbing rapidly toward forty years of age, played a solid game for the Royals, keeping them close during the first quarter with 10 points and five rebounds. Part of Green's success was due to DeBusschere's early foul trouble. Green was being guarded by Bradley and was the first player in some time to really tear Dollar Bill apart offensively.

As if Tuesday night's cardiac game wasn't enough, the Knicks did it again on the tube last night, finally beating the Bucks, 96–95. Bradley was the hero in this one, hitting a shot from the left side with 11 seconds left to win the game. Walt Frazier pulled a groin muscle and sat out half the last quarter, leaving it to Mike Riordan to play sterling defense on Flynn Robinson (who scored 30 points in the game) during the final 11 seconds. Mike forced the Buck sharp-shooter to take a fall away jumper from the foul line, not quite the shot he wanted. Dick Barnett took the rebound and salted away the game by clutching the ball.

Lew Alcindor played a fine game—his best of the season against the Knicks. He scored 25 points and for the first time against New York was an intimidating force on defense. Once again the woes of Willis Reed, only slightly perceptible in the statistics but blatantly obvious to the fans, might have contributed to Lew's apparent improvement. On the other hand, the fact that the season is thirty games old must have helped age Big Lew too.

The Knickerbockers now stand at 27–3, having climbed back up to .900 with their win last night. Tonight they play at Seattle, three games in three nights in three cities spread over 3,000 miles. Saturday night they return to the Garden to play Philadelphia, which battled them to the wire at the Spectrum in their only meeting before the Knicks pulled it out. The road to greatness gets tougher and tougher, as every team in the league looks for ways to beat Holzman's crew. With the early-season pace they established, the Knicks have forced their fans to expect incredible performances, not just a winning record. With the Mets and Jets having already won world championships, the great heritage of the Giants and Yankees, and the Rangers currently unbeaten in fourteen games and in first place, the Knicks are competing in a rough environment. The victories are coming harder, the last two defeats have come within ten days, and Frazier and Reed are physically not up to par. The measure of their mettle lies ahead.

DARRALL IMHOFF

The Philadelphia 76ers responded to my request for interviews by providing a roster of the team, including home addresses and phone numbers. I dropped Darrall Imhoff a note, requesting an interview and telling him I would call to confirm it. He was quite friendly on the phone, agreeing readily to meet me at the Statler-Hilton during the afternoon before the game with the Knicks tonight.

Billy Cunningham, Imhoff's roommate, wasn't going to let me in until it was established that I was an approved guest of Imhoff's. I walked in to find them both in boxer shorts, stretched out on their beds. Imhoff was having a telephone conversation, apparently going over the 76ers' road schedule with some fan somewhere who was also a friend. Cunningham was totally immersed in the Liberty Bowl game on television, in which Colorado ultimately beat Alabama and won a dollar for the star 76er forward, who had made the same token wager against the Raiders in their game with the Chiefs. (For the record, these wagers were made with a friend, not a gambler.) This is being written at halftime, and Oakland is beating Kansas City, 3–0. Billy indicated he thought that would happen—he just wanted to break even.

Darrall Imhoff is an extremely friendly and intelligent man. He is easy to interview, finding it no imposition to expand his answers to cover the full range of a question. He is a solid basketball player whose strengths—setting picks, playing defense, and passing—go largely unnoticed by many fans. Yet he seems happy with his job and did not mention himself among the players he thinks do not get the recognition they deserve. In his view, Chet Walker, Satch Sanders, Bailey Howell, and the Van Arsdale twins are the least appreciated, though talented, players in the NBA by the fans and the press.

Imhoff started his career with the Knicks in 1960 after playing with an NCAA champion at California. "I wouldn't wish it on anybody to start out with New York," he said, an understandable reaction to the two years he spent in a Knickerbocker uniform. The Knicks were a high-scoring loser then, with Guerin and Naulls to collect the points and the fans' adulation. I mentioned to Imhoff that he didn't get as many assists when he was with the Knicks as he does today.

Was that a result of an adjustment he had made? "How can you get assists when you don't touch the ball? I never got the ball with the Knicks at all. Guerin would bring it up and shoot it, or Naulls would shoot." But Imhoff's sympathy for ballplayers who must start their pro careers in New York runs even deeper. "Eastern fans bet the spread and are extremely concerned at the end of a ballgame with their money. Western fans are more concerned with rooting for their own team." In this regard, Imhoff took a lot of knocks from the old Garden faithful, even though he admits rue-fully that they began to give him some credit when he started to play more in his second, and last, year with the Knicks.

Imhoff also admits that Eastern fans may know the game better than Western fans and that this increased knowledge is in part a cause of their seemingly unending discontent. Although he didn't say so explicitly, the implication was strong that his favorite fans were in Los Angeles, and that Laker announcer Chick Hearn was at least partially responsible for the tenor of Laker supporters. "Chick goes out of his way to be fair and to give credit to a ballplayer, not knocking him. King, however, the San Francisco announcer, is terribly biased. That affects the fan's reactions."

To an extent, Imhoff is an organization man. In response to a question about gambling by NBA players, he responded excitedly, "There better *not* be. Man, this is our livelihood. You'd have to be pretty stupid to risk ruining your liveli-hood." He is fully aware that there have been two scandals in basketball over the past twenty years, and it is clear that the prospect of the game's ruin as a spectator sport is up-setting emotionally as well as financially. On the other hand, he appraises his situation and his experiences honestly, without mincing words when he has a criticism.

Carl Braun, Imhoff's coach with the Knicks, was merely "an excuse for a coach." Said Imhoff, "In fairness to Carl, it's rough to be as close to the players as you are as a player and then try to coach them. I think DeBusschere had that trouble too." Imhoff feels that an ability to handle men is as important as knowledge of the game. Pete Newell, his coach at California and currently the general manager of the San Diego Rockets, was the best he ever played for. Jack Ramsey, his coach now at Philadelphia, rates a close second. "There could be a problem on this club, with so many good ballplayers on the bench. When Luke (Jackson) is healthy, there's myself, Jones, Hetzel, Guokas—guys who could be playing on other clubs." The inference is that there is no problem with Philadelphia.

I asked Imhoff about the league's officiating. Cunningham looked away from the football game he was watching and reminded his roommate of the $250 fine for criticizing the officiating. Imhoff smiled and formed his answer around the rules. "Let's just say that the officiating *had* to suffer because we lost four experienced refs to the ABA this year. It takes time for the new guys to get adjusted." Adjustment, rather than ability, is the current problem with the officiating, he feels.

The NBA players are a "close-knit" group because there are so few of them (twelve to each of the fourteen teams). They know each other and they know what's going on all over the league. In response to that, I asked Imhoff what happened to Walt Bellamy, once one of the best centers in the game and now playing second-string to Otto Moore at Detroit. "Just not putting out," Imhoff replied, although he agreed that there wasn't much of that. Most NBA players were concerned enough about their performance to give the required effort all the time.

I always wondered why some top college ballplayers didn't make it in pro ball. For example, I suggested Barry Kramer, one time stalwart of NYU. Imhoff added Gary Bradds, who has done fairly well in the ABA but "did nothing" in a stint with Baltimore. "There are several reasons. One is just the physical contact. The pro game is a lot rougher. Secondly, you aren't seeing a good big man just once in a while. Here, everybody is real big and real quick. Third, remember that Lew Alcindor has already played a college schedule (thirty games). I think he's getting tired. You know, it's not fair to expect as much of him as people do. It takes a while to make the adjustment."

Will Lew be the best someday? "Maybe, but I'm not sure. Right now, Wilt is still the best. He's so much stronger. But Lew is quick and he's got all sorts of moves and spins." Cunningham suggested that the 76ers had pretty good success getting Lew to go to the baseline. Imhoff and Cunningham agreed that the 6-footer from the baseline was one of the toughest shots in basketball, it being an "in-between" shot. There is a tendency to shoot it short.

The toughest center for Imhoff? No hesitation—"Nate Thurmond of San Francisco." But he'd said Wilt was the best. "He is, but Thurmond has those long arms, and he goes so hard at *both* ends of the court. Willis Reed gives me trouble too. He's even stronger than Thurmond, and he's left-handed. But Thurmond is the roughest."

I asked Imhoff if he thought the 76ers had gotten a break in the schedule, having only played the Knicks once so far this season. The Knicks have been hot—maybe they'll be returning to the mortals.

"No, I don't think so. We always play the Knicks tough because we match up well against them. That's the real key to pro ball, the matchups. We played them in exhibition and it went overtime, and we had a squeaker against them that we lost in Philly. They don't have anybody who can stop Billy." Who can, I wondered? Imhoff smiled. "He jumps over the little forwards and goes around the big ones. He's awful tough." Cunningham didn't react; his eyes were riveted on the television set.

I mentioned to Cunningham that I might like to talk to him the same way later on in the season. He nodded. I asked him about jumping to the ABA and he said, "Yup, I'm going to do it." Why? Both Imhoff and Cunningham laughed. "Why do you think we're in this game?" Darrall asked. "To make money for our families while we can play and to provide for them afterward." Cunningham pointed out that a ballplayer's active life is pretty short. But the future move hasn't affected his play, nor the team's performance, in any way he could see. Imhoff was fully in agreement.

I will see tonight's game differently on the basis of the afternoon's conversation. Darrall Imhoff is a friendly, helpful person in the top echelons of his profession, a starting center on a strong professional basketball team. He is not an oaf who happens to be slightly longer than his contemporaries, and whatever contribution his height has made to his success is matched by his awareness and his own interest. He explained that the players can avoid interviews if they want to because they are contracted only to play basketball and make a limited number of appearances for the club. He obviously chooses not to avoid them, but he grants them in a manner that makes clear his desire to assist someone else who is doing his job, not for his personal aggrandizement or gain. He is forgiven even for not thinking New York fans are the best there are. Maybe he is even right.

DECEMBER 16

For the first time this season the Knicks will take the court tonight attempting to snap a streak. Not until 32 games had gone by this season did the Knicks lose two straight, but Saturday night's defeat to the Philadelphia 76ers was the third in four games after only two defeats in the first 29 games. Holzman, typically, said Saturday night he would begin to worry about it on Monday. Each fan and news-paper writer is proposing a theory as to why the Superteam has slumped. It is unlikely that the team that has stumbled for a week now is the real Knicks. However, it is also unlikely that the real Knicks are a 27–2 team. The answer lies in be-tween. The Knicks hope to begin describing that answer against Atlanta tonight.

The Hawks have met the Knicks twice, once in the Garden and once in Atlanta. Both times the Knicks ran away to victory. The *Post* reports tonight that Richie Guerin cannot believe the Knicks are in a slump. They must have appeared incapable of it when he saw them.

But while the loss to Seattle last Thursday night could be blamed on fatigue and the absence of Walt Frazier from the lineup, Saturday's loss was the effort of a team in a slump. The shooting was miserable by all hands, starting five and substitutes. The aggressive team defense, hurt by the op-position strategy of taking Walt Frazier away from the ball, has fallen apart and simply does not produce turnovers like it once did. Both DeBusschere and Bradley are failing on the offensive board, so the Knicks' bad shooting is not but-tressed by extra attempts at the basket. Worse yet, the Knicks are failing in the second half, something that a deep team is not supposed to do. Against Philadelphia, a lead was built in the second quarter, partly squandered by halftime, and completely dissipated by a 10-point Philadelphia burst in the third quarter. Like Detroit had the night the Knicks lost the big streak, the 76ers won pulling away.

Things have gotten to the point that grumbling can now be heard among the customers directed against specific players. The complaints in my section seem to be directed against Mike Riordan. The Knicks are still above any "booing," but Max, the fellow next to me on the left, is sure the Knicks should move Bradley to backcourt and bring Russell or Stallworth in at forward to improve their shooting when Barnett or Frazier is resting. He has no faith in Riordan's offensive ability—despite the 27 points Mike notched in Seattle when Frazier was hurt. I don't doubt that Max has been thinking these things all season, but they have surfaced now that the locals have dropped a couple of games.

The point spread doesn't seem to be severely affected yet, although it will have to be if the Knicks don't show an early-season effort soon. The morning line on tonight's game shows the Knicks by 8½ over the 19–11 Hawks, perhaps on the strength of the Knicks' earlier efforts against them. Max said that the Knicks were favored by from 7 to 10 against the 76ers on Saturday night despite the Knicks' slump and what Darrall Imhoff calls "the good matchups" of the two teams.

Not that it is all that glum. The Knicks are 27–5, 6½ games better than second-place Baltimore. The two major physical problems, Willis Reed's toe and Walt Frazier's groin injury, are considerably improved with the couple of days of rest since Saturday's game. Mike Riordan *did* score 27 points on Thursday, which has to do wonders for his confidence and, consequently, his ability in the backcourt. It is just a matter of picking up those five delicate pieces—Barnett, Bradley, DeBusschere, Frazier, and Reed—and putting them back together again. There is little doubt it will happen before too much damage is done. The only question right now is if it will happen tonight.

But the New York fandom and press are clearly spoiled. Pity the Jets, who finished the season at 10–4 and in first place in their division but had the query "What's wrong?" hurled at them all season because they did not win every game by fourteen touchdowns. Perhaps pity the Rangers, who went on a binge of their own and have now dropped two out of three. They remain in first place, but their non-losing standard has slipped slightly. But mostly, pity the Knicks, who made the mistake of convincing us all that they were the greatest combination of talents ever clothed in shorts and placed on hardwood and who are now suspect if they lose even one ballgame. In New York, success has the built-in disadvantage of decreasing your margin for error.

DONNIE MAY

It is difficult to imagine how many obstacles are placed in the path of an unknown author trying to interview the New York Knicks. I called Jim Wergeles, who carries the title "director of publicity," in September, explaining that I was going to do a book and requesting help in interviewing the Knicks. He promised to call back, and didn't.

I called again, and this time I was told that I needed a letter from my publisher, since the Knicks were so deluged with interview demands that they had had to screen out the phonies. My editor at Prentice-Hall sent the required note.

Still I was put off. The season was just beginning and Coach Holzman wanted to make sure everything got off on the right foot. No interviews for a while. They would call me. They did not.

Finally, last week I got some sort of satisfaction out of Mr. Wergeles, who explained how extensive the demands had been on the ballplayers' time. *Life* had done a piece, as had *Time, Newsweek,* and *Sports Illustrated.* The ballplayers were tired and overinterviewed. However, he could arrange for me to steal a couple of minutes before a ballgame to speak to the players individually, and since my only timetable was that I wanted to interview everybody before the season ended, he thought he could accommodate me. I was to call him Monday preceding the game with Atlanta on Tuesday and he would set me up.

Meanwhile, somebody had told me that the man to speak

to at the Garden was not Jim Wergeles at all, but Frank Blauschild, director of public relations. Sure enough, when I called for Wergeles on Monday, Blauschild picked up the phone. I informed him of Wergeles' tentative commitment, so Blauschild gave me my instructions. I was to pick up a press pass at Window 21 and use it to be admitted to the press-table area before six o'clock. He would arrange for me to speak "to someone."

I picked up my pass, which was waiting for me as promised. Walking around the building to the entrance marked "8 Pennsylvania Plaza," as Blauschild instructed, I noticed how little traffic there was around the Garden. I realized I hadn't ever been near the building except within an hour of gametime. The door opened on a barren lobby where a uniformed man ripped my ticket and instructed me to take the elevator to the fifth floor. I remembered that Chick Hearn used to complain on the air about his broadcasting position in the Garden being on the ninth floor, with the basketball court on the fifth floor. Now I understood what he meant. The elevator was full of people who knew each other—ushers, vendors, officials. They traded hellos as I tried very hard to look inconspicuous, difficult when your hair is longer than everybody else's by several inches. I clutched the ticket stub in my pocket to make sure I didn't lose it. I still had my ticket to the game, but I didn't want to lose my evidence of authority to be in special places at special times in this very special building.

Leaving the elevator, I simply followed my nose until the cold concrete insides of the arena gave way to the glittering amphitheater, or what the signs called the "rotunda." An elderly man was labeling all the seats at the press table. Before speaking to him, I combed the tags to see if my working press "courtside" ticket entitled me to a seat so close to the floor. My name wasn't listed. I looked up and spotted my regular seat from the ring of orange thirty rows or so above me.

On the floor, a game between Cardinal Spellman and Cardinal Hayes was in the first half. Back in the old Garden days I used to go to Knick games early to see these high school games, which sometimes featured Power Memorial and Lew Alcindor. Nobody on the court on Tuesday looked like a potential NBA superstar.

I asked the old man whether Mr. Blauschild was around. He said that neither Blauschild nor Wergeles were expected until shortly before gametime. I nodded, somehow having figured that they would have forgotten me. I sat at the press table, watching the high school game and trying to figure out how to keep my eyes peeled for Blauschild and Wergeles when I had no idea what they looked like.

I had drifted into a stoned reverie, mesmerized by the court action within the empty magnificence of the arena, when the old man pointed out Blauschild and Wergeles coming into the "rotunda" from the opposite side of the court. I walked around the floor to intercept them. Blauschild told me to have Wergeles take care of me.

Now, Wergeles hadn't even known I was there, not having spoken to me for almost a week. Like a good p.r. man. however, he made a fast recovery and took me into the locker room. There were two Knick players in there—Willis Reed was fully in uniform and sitting on one bench. Donnie May was in streetclothes (with the exception of his shoes, which had already been kicked off) and sitting on another bench autographing a basketball with a felt-tipped pen. Wergeles looked around, hesitated a moment, then introduced me to Donnie May.

If May were only playing more regularly and were single, he would have the equipment to challenge Joe Namath of the Jets and Rod Gilbert of the Rangers on the bachelor circuit. He is good-looking and smiles easily. His answers to my questions indicate that he is happy with his lot, even as twelfth man on a twelve-man squad.

I told May that Darrall Imhoff had said that he wouldn't

wish it on any player to start his career in New York. May misunderstood my question at first and self-consciously said he couldn't speak "firsthand" on what it is like to be a starting player with New York. When I restated the question, he relaxed.

"It's one of the *best* places from what I hear. They had a losing team when Darrall played here, didn't they? Maybe that had something to do with it, but the way we've been going, it's great. I knew Arlen Bockhorn, who used to play with Cincinnati and he *always* wanted to play in New York. I guess it's because the pay is better, the opportunities are greater."

How about the fans?

"Well, first of all, there's more of 'em in New York than anywhere else. I think they're also much more knowledgeable. You know, most places they know to applaud when the home team scores a basket. Here you can get cheered for anything—a good pass, a steal, a defensive play. That adds to your incentive, because you know if you play well it will be recognized. I think that's how it should be."

May felt that it was definitely an advantage for the Knicks to play at home, even though at the time of the interview four of their five defeats had taken place at the Garden. "I'd say it doesn't make too much difference where we play on the road," he said. "Philly and Baltimore are probably the toughest fans, but they're tough teams anyway. Except Boston. It seems like we have as many fans up there as they do. Playing in Boston is almost like playing at home."

That was peculiar. I had neglected to mention it, but Darrall Imhoff had said that Boston fans were the most partisan in the East, despite the point-spread gambling that took place along the Atlantic coast. "Boston fans are really *Boston* fans," Imhoff had said. Maybe his situation is different because he had contested national championships with Boston as a member of the Lakers and then Philadelphia.

Maybe a large crowd of New Yorkers turned out when the Knicks were in town. In any case, May and Imhoff were at odds on that point.

While I was talking to May, Bill Hosket, Johnny Warren, and Dave DeBusschere made their way into the locker room. Hosket had completely changed into uniform before the brief conversation with May was completed. Over an hour to go before the game and both Hosket and Reed were suited up.

I wandered back outside to watch the conclusion of the Spellman-Hayes game and saw a few of the Atlanta Hawks wandering around, also in uniform. Dave Newmark, the brash 7-foot center who had played with Columbia, was talking with a pair of shaggy-haired fans who might have been fellow alumni. Butch Beard and Gary Gregor were also wandering around. Richie Guerin sat down near the court and was besieged by old friends from the Knick brass and autograph hunters.

Meanwhile, Knicks kept coming in. Cazzie Russell walked in with Dave Stallworth, and both were obviously displeased that the court was being used by the high school teams. "How the hell we gonna shoot around with them out there, Caz?" Stallworth asked. Russell was too busy being led away for a WLIB radio interview to answer.

JANUARY 23

I have managed to get this far without ever letting on just exactly who Mike Shatzkin is, partly because I didn't think it was important and partly because I hoped you might all know by the time the book comes out. However, this is the first entry in over a month, and the reason for that is couched in my own identity. So before I catch you up with the Knicks, I will catch you up with me.

I am twenty-two years old (which tells you my generation), and during the three-week road trip the Knicks are concluding tonight in Chicago, I was in Los Angeles recording my second album of my own material (which tells you my "bag"). The first one was done last summer, and in the months since then I have lived with the fact that it wasn't quite as good as I can do and I've been itching to get back into the recording studio. The only two breaks in the season, however, were ten days in November and three weeks in January. This dictated that the album would be done when it was.

The preparation for the album and my physical relocation to the West Coast for three weeks necessitated my merely writing notes about the Knicks in the interim (these other entries were *really* written on the dates given). I saw the Knicks play (and lose) in San Diego and caught a nationally televised Knick–Celtic game from Boston (which they also lost), the only opportunities I had to see them while I was away. I learned some interesting things while I was away, however, such as that people are not nearly as impressed by the Knicks' brilliance in other cities as we are here in New York. That is not unreasonable. Their current record of 38–11 is not so much better than Milwaukee's 34–16—or even Baltimore's 31–19—that a fall from first place before season's end is inconceivable.

A basketball season is much longer than I had ever remembered it being, but I never *thought* about one so carefully before. Think of the stages the Knicks have gone through even up to the point before Christmas, when I last made an entry. The season started with that fabulous flourish: 5 wins, then 1 loss, and then 18 wins. That took us through more than six weeks of action, including a heavy concentration of home games followed by a rough road trip. And the Knicks were 23–1. I remember wondering whether they would lose five games all year. In the beginning the margins of victory were incredible, beating the point spread far more often than not. That gradually began to change. Then, when last I wrote, the Knicks had fallen into a bit of a losing streak. They lost a heartbreaker to Atlanta (in overtime) on the night I interviewed Donnie May. The ship got righted in Chicago the following Friday night, and the Knicks blew Baltimore off the floor on the following Saturday night (the Bullets always seem to be a tonic). Then the Knicks got a gentle five-day break to get ready for the most excruciating road trip of the season. It went like this:

Thursday night they beat Detroit in the Garden; Friday night they lost to the Lakers in Los Angeles; Saturday night they beat Seattle in Vancouver, British Columbia; Sunday night they beat Phoenix at Phoenix; and Tuesday afternoon they beat Chicago at the Garden to close out 1969. The loss was directly attributable to two things—fatigue in the second half (the game started at eleven New York time, and an airplane ride following a night game is hardly the way to adjust to a time difference) and a fabulous shooting spree by Jerry West. The victories that started and ended the marathon were most notable, however.

The Detroit game was a nip-and-tuck affair that saw Detroit build up a substantial lead in the fourth quarter. Finally, with a solid spurt, the Knicks pulled to within 1 and had the ball with 30 seconds to go. Bill Bradley hit a jumper on the side with 15 seconds left to bring the lead back home, but Detroit had 15 seconds to turn it around. With 3 seconds left Walt Bellamy got the ball tight against the left-hand corner of the Detroit forecourt and started a drive that culminated in a bucket with 1 second to go. The Knicks called time-out.

Everybody in the Garden knew what the Knicks had to do. A perfect pass from out of bounds at midcourt by Walt Frazier did it. Willis Reed was freed by a pick on the out-of-bounds play, went up as high as he could, caught Frazier's pass, and dropped it through the hoop. The buzzer sounded as the ball hit the cords and the Knicks had won their third straight. Nobody could have written a better script for Christmas night.

The Chicago game was reminiscent of the earlier victories, back during the Golden Era of the season when nobody came close to the Knicks. Willis again led the onslaught, piling up over 20 points and twenty rebounds, and the Knicks let everybody play in a 116–96 rout. Actually, it wasn't quite that close.

But just before the Knicks and I went on our road trips, things turned for the worse again. On Friday night, January 2, the Knicks went into Milwaukee and couldn't stop Lew Alcindor. The old Bruin pumped 43 points through and the Bucks ran away. The Knicks had beaten the Bucks in four previous games, on three occasions holding them under 100 points. Those were the only three games in which Milwaukee didn't top the century. Coming on more strongly since Alcindor has adjusted to his new teammates, however, they appeared to be posing a threat to the Knicks' dominance of the Eastern Division. The Knicks failed to beat them, failed to hold them under 100 points, and certainly did nothing to dispel the threat.

The following night the Boston Celtics came in for the last home game before the Ice Capades moved into the Garden, and the Knicks lost again. They just didn't have it as an inferior team outran, outshot, and outrebounded them. It was a helluva note to leave home on.

The first night I was in Los Angeles I went to see the Lakers play Phoenix at the Forum. The game, won by the Lakers fairly easily, was a dreadful bore. The Los Angeles fans, treated to a typically brilliant performance by Jerry West and with a team battling to overcome Atlanta for first place in the Western Division, seemed not to care very much. The Forum organist played many of the same riffs that Eddie Layton uses to arouse the Garden fans, but to no avail. With 11,000 locals in attendance, all cheering for the home side and unaware of any point spread, there was less enthusiasm than at an exciting funeral. It just wasn't the same. I wanted to go back again, because the great number of Laker games I had attended before becoming such a constant attendee in New York, didn't play back quite that quietly on the tapes in my mind. However, Holiday on Ice moved into the Forum while the Ice Capades hit the Garden, so the Lakers also went on the road.

The next day I was in San Diego to work with my lead guitarist on some material, so I stopped at the Sports Arena there to get tickets for the Knick–San Diego game scheduled for the following Saturday night. The arena is attractive from the outside, with plenty of parking, and I expected not to be able to get decent seats for such an attraction as the Knicks. Any fears I had were completely unwarranted. With the top price in San Diego only $5, I picked up four in the front row at side court at the box office. I guess ticket scalping must be a hard way to earn a living in San Diego.

During that week, between the time I bought the tickets and the San Diego game, the Knicks marched through Baltimore on their way to San Francisco the way Sherman had marched through Atlanta on his way to the sea. They decimated the Bullets again. San Francisco fell twice in three days, and the Knicks had a brand-new three-game winning streak when we all arrived in San Diego on Saturday night. Being somewhat of a vocal fan (which makes me stand out in most places) and having somewhat longish hair (which makes me stand out in San Diego, particularly at the San Diego Sports Arena), the people around me gleaned very quickly that "an enemy was in the midst of the section." It was murder. The Knicks fell behind in the third quarter, obviously tired, and Elvin Hayes never let them catch up. Nate Bowman was doing his thing—picking up fouls right and left and angrily stalking the officials—but it wasn't nearly as amusing as it is in New York.

The entire tenor of the San Diego crowd reminded me of my old high school basketball games. The air was filled with such expletives as "Let's not throw it away" and "Darn it, we need some teamwork, Elvin." I am *not* kidding. When one fan behind me leaned forward to make some sarcastic remark about a pass Frazier had thrown away, I started to explain that Bradley had been bumped by Hayes when he headed for the basket and the spot the ball had passed through. I realized that there was no hope. Picks, screens, defense—they were way beyond most of these fans. I began to understand what Donnie May had meant about the so-phistication of the New York fans—"most places they know to applaud when the home team scores a basket." Was he ever correct with *that* evaluation! I thought about the people in my section back in New York: Max, who bet the games and could feel the pulse of every game; Dan, whom I always felt interpreted the game simply but who saw the good pick, the smart foul, the solid defensive play; and that fellow in front of me I didn't get along with at the beginning of the season but with whom I have since concocted elaborate theories about why Cincinnati always gives the Knicks a tough game. I think *all* of them would have been equally shocked in San Diego.

After losing in San Diego, the Knicks beat Detroit and Phoenix before the nationally televised game against Boston last Sunday. The now lowly Celtics became the first team this year to defeat the Knicks for a second time and took the lead in the season series, 2–1. The Knicks play the Celtics again this Sunday afternoon at Boston and next Tuesday night at the Garden, so they have a chance to take that lead back. Maybe Coach Tommy Heinsohn has Red Holzman's number.

The bright note for this week, so far, was the All-Star

game in Philly last Tuesday. Holzman coached the East, which won with large thanks to game MVP Willis Reed. Frazier also started, and DeBusschere was chosen for the squad. Bradley and Barnett didn't make it, as much because the limit was three representatives from one team as anything else.

And that brings us completely up to date with the Knicks. Tonight they have a televised game at Chicago to complete the road trip, and tomorrow they finally come home, against San Diego. They stand at 38–11, with eighteen home games and fifteen road games to go. DeBusschere's back hurts, which might keep him out tonight, but the injury is not deemed serious. Willis Reed has had a stomach ache, but extensive tests earlier this week disclosed nothing seriously wrong with him. Other teams haven't been quite as lucky— Nate Thurmond hurt his knee and is out for the season, and just when San Francisco got Jerry Lucas back from his injury. Thurmond, who has been injured often throughout his career, says he is going to call it quits. Chamberlain is out of the cast but nobody knows when he'll be back, and Baylor has been hobbling for the Lakers. Even without the return of Phil Jackson—which was supposed to have happened and hasn't (and which nobody seems to talk about much anymore)—the Knicks are relatively healthy. I feel like the season is starting all over again, so much has happened since I was last at the Garden. Maybe they're not too tired to feel the same way!

BOB WOLFF

I spoke to Bob Wolff on the Garden floor while I was waiting for Frank Blauschild ten days ago. Wolff responded pleasantly to my request for an interview and agreed to grant me as much time as I wanted. When I called him the

Monday following, as we had agreed, he pleaded for a week's postponement because he had just lost his secretary and was headed for a week's road trip. However, he made it clear that he would make time for me immediately if it were crucial. I assured him that I could comfortably wait a week, so we settled on a date the following Monday. That was yesterday.

I had never been inside the 2 Pennsylvania Plaza building, which houses the Madison Square Garden and NBA offices and was built as part of the Madison Square Garden Center complex. Simply following Wolff's instructions, however, I found the Garden offices on the eighteenth floor. After a few minutes, Wolff came out to meet me.

"Would you mind waiting while I make a couple of calls?" he asked, explaining the duress he works under while in-between secretaries.

I amused myself by letting my eyes wander around Wolff's small rectangular office, noting that he had large envelopes with the name of an NBA team on each one on a table near the office doorway. Also on the table were two record albums, leaned up against the wall so the titles were visible. One was "Great Sounds from Madison Square Garden" and the other was an album by Everett Dirksen.

Wolff's desk was cluttered with letters from fans and Knickerbocker and Ranger home programs. He does the television play-by-play for the basketball and hockey games, keeping him on the road a great deal of the time during the winter sports season. And he obviously spends a great deal of his nonbroadcasting time keeping informed for his shows.

Wolff finished his last call and suggested the bowling lanes' coffee shop in the building for a bite of lunch. On the way down in the elevator, he clasped his hands together in front of him as if he were about to kneel in prayer. Perhaps this is a habit he has cultivated as a television announcer to keep his hands from committing distracting misdemeanors against his monologue. When the elevator door opened in the lobby, Wolff began to chronicle his career.

At Duke, before World War II, he had been a baseball player before a broken ankle sidelined him in his sophomore year. He started sitting in the booth during the radio broadcasts of the Duke games and his voluntary commentary was so popular that the CBS affiliate that carried the games offered him a paying position in the booth. When he asked his coach, former Philadelphia A's pitcher Jack Coombs, whether to take the job, he was told, "Bob, if you want to make it to the major leagues, just keep talking." Wolff laughed and explained that he has been talking ever since.

After World War II, during which he followed duty in the South Pacific by working for the Navy Department in Washington, Wolff applied for the job as TV commentator for the Washington Senator broadcasts. At that time, TV was only a baby, and the veteran Senator radiomen were sticking to their jobs. Several years later, having been the TV man since Washington started videoing the games, Wolff moved up into full partnership in the broadcasts when the TV and radio rights were bought by the same sponsor.

Wolff was building a name for himself in Washington, handling the basketball Caps of the old Basketball Association of America (the forerunner of the NBA) and the hockey broadcasts when Washington had a hockey team. In addition, he started a subsidiary venture of sports films for television and wrote a column to be distributed to the cities where the films were shown. By the middle of the 1950s, through the same Washington Senator sponsor, he started doing New York Knick and Ranger telecasts.

"I used to commute then," Wolff recalled. "I lived in Washington and would only fly to New York for a day at a time to do the Saturday night Knick games and the midweek Ranger games. Nobody in Washington knew I was working in New York and the New York people didn't know where I came from. It was working out very well, establishing me in both cities."

When the American League expanded and the old Senators' franchise moved to Minneapolis–St. Paul, Bob Wolff went with it. "Things were getting a little ridiculous then. I had a home in Washington, worked frequently in New York during the winter, and spent the summers in Minnesota. That was when I decided to quit the Minnesota job."

There was discussion with the New York Mets' franchise about Wolff taking over as their broadcaster, but Wolff ultimately signed to do the NBC Game of the Week and his family moved to Scarsdale, New York, where they still live.

"The NBC job, combined with doing the Madison Square Garden telecasts, created a problem. My oldest son, Bobby, was captain of his football team in his senior year and I didn't get to see one game. I vowed then that I would work out a way to see his younger brother, Ricky, play all his games. When the contract with NBC terminated, I worked out an arrangement to become the p.r. man for Madison Square Garden Corporation, giving up the telecasts. For three years I saw every football game that Ricky played at Edgemont High, and saw him play baseball at Edgemont and Bobby pitch at Princeton. We've always been a closely knit sporting family, so it was very important to me. This year, with Ricky graduated (he's at Harvard) and Bobby pitching his last season at Princeton, I was free to go back to the mike. I was offered the opportunity to do the telecasts and the job as executive assistant to Irving Mitchell Felt, the president of the Madison Square Garden Corporation. Mr. Felt agreed to give me the time I needed to prepare properly for the broadcasts. It has worked out very well for me."

Wolff's duties as p.r. man were considerable. He handled the job at the time that the Madison Square Garden operation was moving from Fiftieth Street to the new Garden

72

complex. "The hours were long," Wolff recalls, but he takes pride in the job he did.

Bob Wolff is a very proud man, but in the sort of way that at the same time makes him a very kind man. His professional accomplishments are legion, and in the field of his strongest personal interest. He is secure in his stature and his versatility and, apparently freed from the insecurity that marks the sports and entertainment business, has time for concern about others.

I asked Wolff whether he felt he could do anything on the air to ameliorate a situation such as Howard Komives had in New York. Komives is a solid professional guard who was an amazingly prolific scorer at Bowling Green. During the last two years of the several he spent with the Knicks, the fans treated him unmercifully. I pointed out to Wolff that this *had* to affect Komives' play, it *had* to affect the team's play and it probably was a factor in his being dealt to Detroit last winter in the trade that brought Dave DeBusschere to New York.

Wolff agreed that the Komives situation was difficult, but pointed out that there was little he could do to help. "If Komives fumbles the ball on TV, all I can say is, 'Komives fumbled the ball.' However, if I were to say, 'Komives fumbled it *again*, fans,' that would be something else. I wouldn't do that. But I can't deny what's on the screen."

A more difficult situation, Wolff feels, is the Mystery of Walt Bellamy. He expressed concern about the bad press Bellamy gets and the oft-repeated evaluation—repeated to me by Darrall Imhoff—that Bellamy doesn't "put out."

"Is that really true?" Wolff asked. "How can we tell? I'd say that's a pretty serious knock. It might just be that Bellamy is slow, doesn't have real good hands. When he first came into the league, he was a real big man, which may be why he scored so much. Now he's just a normal center."

Wolff has some very definite thoughts about his responsibilities as a broadcaster. He indicated that it makes little difference to him what sport he is doing, since the thrill lies in the "tension of the event." He added, "Even when you're doing a dog show, which I have done, you are serving as the eyes and ears, the focal point, for a lot of people who are very concerned about how this thing will turn out. I like baseball, football, hockey, pro and college basketball. All of them have this same element."

On the other hand, Wolff feels that crowd noise and excitement are very important tools and guides for the broadcaster. "When I'm doing a game, I'm just a fan. A good announcer reflects the crowd. I can't yell if the crowd is quiet. If it's a good play, you can get excited, 'Good play!' But it is very hard to generate excitement if none is there. If you take a baseball game on a Tuesday afternoon with 5,000 people in the stands, it could be the best game in the world, but it is hard to make it exciting. If it's Friday night with a full house, the same stadium, same teams, it is much easier."

Did this mean that his own broadcasting had improved as the Knicks and Rangers had become winners?

"Probably," he said. "You saw that mail I had upstairs." Wolff had shown me a letter from a young fan who was as excited with Wolff as he was with the Rangers and Knicks. "Most of it is like that these days."

Wolff has some interesting notions about broadcasting basketball in New York too. "Rightly or wrongly, New Yorkers seem to feel that basketball is a New York game which has been adopted by the rest of the country. When I broadcast to New York, I know that every coach, player, would-be player, is tuned in. I can't bluff these people. They know the game much too well. They appreciate the game here as a performance, the same way you would appreciate a stage show, watching the lighting, the sets, the costumes, the acting. Of course, the Knick fans come to see the Knicks win, but they stay until the end of the game because they get excited about the steals, the fast breaks. In most cities, far more attention is paid to whether the team wins or loses."

At that point, we headed back up to his office. As he passed through the Garden Center lobby, he was stopped several times by people with friendly hellos, and he seemed to know them all. I felt comfortable enough with him by this time to discuss my problem of interviewing the athletes.

"It is difficult," he said. "This p.r. department gets beholden to the regular writers who have been traveling with the team for some time. They wonder why, if anything being done on the Knicks is worth anything, the regulars aren't doing it. And the regulars themselves aren't too friendly about new people breaking into the group." I thought about a phone call I had made to Leonard Lewin of the *Post,* asking for an interview. Lewin is never in the office, so the message was going to be passed on. He never called back.

I wondered whether it might be possible to follow Wolff on a road trip to see what is involved in doing a telecast of a Knick game. He pondered the question, but only briefly. "Sure, I think that could be arranged. I could let you look through my notes so that if we got separated for a while you would be able to see what I use to get ready." We agreed on next week's game at Philadelphia. I am to tell Blauschild that I "would like to make the trip." Wolff assured me that the Knicks should take care of the rest.

Having met Bob Wolff and been totally charmed by his sincerity and eagerness to help, I remembered how much I liked his broadcasts when I was a young fan. To some extent, Bob Wolff taught me basketball when I had an awful lot to learn and, if his mail is any barometer, he is doing the same now for many other young Knick fans. Whatever one's personal reaction to Bob Wolff on the air, it is impossible to ignore the diligence with which he does his job. I have written letters to fourteen club publicists, conducted interviews, harassed Blauschild and Wergeles to my own exhaustion, but as yet Wolff is the only person who has shown an excited interest in the book. The fact that he is a busy man and a successful man, has not made him forget that others also have a job to do.

FEBRUARY 3

There have been times this season when you could let a week slide by without writing about basketball and still not have too much to report. I am afraid this was not one of those weeks. Tonight the Knicks carry an eight-game winning streak into their Garden match with San Francisco. All eight have been won since the All-Star break, and on only three days in the last eleven did the Knicks have no game. The local fans have been well-informed about the entire streak, since the four road games of the eight were televised, two by Bob Wolff on local television and two on the ABC Game of the Week.

Chicago fell in Chicago to begin the current streak, as Bill Bradley scored 35 points to lead the Knicks. This marked the professional career high for Bradley, who followed up with a solid scoring effort the next night in the Garden against San Diego. The Chicago game was close until the closing minutes, despite Bradley's effort, but the San Diego game was a rout. Perhaps the Knicks were paying back the Rockets for the defeat they suffered while we were all on the Coast.

The next two victories were over Boston, up there on Sunday and back home on Tuesday. The Tuesday game was noteworthy because the Knickerbockers ran away with it, precipitating nasty "they-pile-it-on" commentary from the Boston press and TV corps. Heinsohn and Havlicek, the Boston coach and star player, however, excused the rout.

Heinsohn particularly praised Willis Reed for putting out 100 percent no matter what the score, and Havlicek acknowledged that the Knicks had a long score to settle with the Celtics. Meanwhile, the New York press defended the Knicks and Coach Holzman by documenting numerous routs that Boston had inflicted during the Bill Russell days.

Bill Bradley injured an ankle against the Celtics and was yanked by Holzman barely a minute after the Garden game with Detroit started on Thursday. It made little difference. Cazzie Russell was a fully acceptable substitute in this game and the two that followed. Donnie May also got some playing time and did well.

Friday night's game at Philadelphia was the most exciting of the streak. The Knicks were down, 50–49, at halftime but took off in the third quarter to open an "insurmountable" lead that Philadelphia almost surmounted. As hot as the Knicks were in the third quarter, were the 76ers in the fourth, but the Knickerbockers eventually prevailed for victory number 6.

Walt Frazier led the rout against Chicago on Saturday night, matching the 35 that Bradley had scored the week before. With the Garden sold out again (the Detroit game is the only one for as long as I can remember that was *not* a sellout, 19,500), the Knicks didn't give the Bulls much of a chance.

At Detroit on Sunday it was Dave DeBusschere's turn to provide offensive lightning, canning a series of jump shots in the stretch that preserved the Knicks' victory. The New Yorkers had fallen behind by as much as 11 in the third quarter, but a "loose-press" defense—working without the foul-plagued Frazier—forced enough turnovers to bring home the money.

The Knicks have apparently put it together again with this streak. All of the starters, especially Willis Reed, are playing consistently well. The team defense, having overcome the problems that offensive adjustments imposed, is working again and coming up with steals. Mike Riordan and Cazzie Russell have provided spark from the bench. The fans seem happy again with their team back over .800 (46–11) and the woes of losing and sloppy play apparently behind them. Milwaukee has continued to win, so they have not lost much ground to the Knicks on this streak (the margin is currently seven games), but the Bullets have slumped so badly that they are no longer a threat.

The big news in pro basketball are the player trades and attempted player trades that beat the February 1 trading deadline. Detroit shipped Eddie Miles—a sharpshooter at forward and guard and popular with Detroit players and fans—to Baltimore for a draft choice and a player of short reputation named Bob Quick. The Pistons also sent Bellamy to Atlanta for a draft choice and a player to be named after the season. The remaining Detroit players were quite upset about the Miles deal, feeling that the Piston management was giving up on this season completely (Detroit is last in the East at 21–37) and making it that much harder on them to finish it up. Piston management, on the other hand, explained that Miles was sure to be lost in the expansion draft (when new teams get to buy players from the established teams after a limited list of protected players is made).

Bob Cousy, having already sent Jerry Lucas to San Francisco, attempted to trade Oscar Robertson to Baltimore. "Cooz" and the Big O have not seen eye-to-eye on the Royals' transition from deliberate basketball to the fast break and, it can be assumed, Cousy felt his authority would be unchallenged if the only remaining big name were traded. What everybody forgot, however, is that Oscar has a no-trade clause in his contract, and he vetoed the Baltimore deal ("What kind of a place is Baltimore?" Oscar said). What the Royals would have gotten in return was not confirmed.

78

Apparently on a tip from Wilt Chamberlain, Warrior owner Franklin Mieuli dealt with Atlanta for the rights to Zelmo Beatty, who had decided to sit out this season and then jump to the ABA. To confuse matters further, there are rumors that the Los Angeles Stars of the ABA are going under and are unable to continue paying Beatty for this season, which he must sit out before he can play for them next year. Mieuli apparently hopes he can convince Beatty to come back with the Warriors. In the meantime, he has taken out his chagrin on former Warrior Coach Bob Lee and replaced him with Al Attles. Lee joins Jack McMahon of San Diego and Johnny Kerr of Phoenix as men who became ex-coaches in 1969–70.

The question of expansion is still up in the air. If there is expansion, it will probably be an addition of four new teams at a cost to the new owners of $3.5 million each. This adds up to a nice round $14 million, which divides evenly by the fourteen teams currently in the NBA. However, three negative votes could still block the expansion, and it is surmised that New York and Milwaukee are strongly against it. If they could pick up a third vote (from somebody who would rather keep all their players than pull in $1 million), there will be no expansion.

And that's not everything that's topsy-turvy. The Lakers, for no apparent reason, have won eight games in a row and taken over first place in the Western Division from Atlanta. Baylor is still sometimes-in, sometimes-out, and Chamberlain isn't back yet. The Hawks, on the other hand, are basically hale and hearty. But there it is, the Lakers in first place. There is still some noise about Chamberlain making it back to the lineup before the playoffs. The Knicks wouldn't be glad to hear that. They, I am sure, anticipate enough trouble from Milwaukee in earning their world championship. More problems aren't necessary.

Tonight the Warriors will feature the first Madison Square

Garden appearance they have made with Jerry Lucas healthy and playing. Luke has other problems, having filed for bankruptcy in the last month. The Warriors, as I mentioned, have difficulties with a new coach and an injured center. Nonetheless, they will probably show up to face the Knicks, and the bookies say they will be the ninth victim of the current streak.

You may remember reading somewhere that the current record for most consecutive victories in professional basketball is eighteen, set by a team called the New York Knickerbockers in 1969.

FEBRUARY 8

The winning streak was expanded to nine games with a trouncing of the undermanned San Francisco Warriors, 118–98, on Tuesday night. Jeff Mullins and Clyde Lee, two men whom the Warriors increasingly depend on with Nate Thurmond hurt, suffered minor injuries in the first half and had to sit out most of the second half. The Knicks did not play as well as they have during the streak, but they opened up a 62–47 halftime lead and coasted home. There was no sellout on Tuesday night, leading one of the local writers to speculate that the fans were bored by the locals' success. This is hardly the case. A crowd of 17,488 hardly indicates rampant disinterest, especially against as uninteresting an opponent as the injury-racked Warriors.

The streak was snapped by Atlanta on the road Wednesday night in a televised game that the Knicks must have been ashamed of. Apparently fighting the fatigue of a strenuous trip South, during which they had to abandon their plans to fly from snowbound La Guardia and shift, after a wait, to Kennedy, the Knicks were no match for the Hawks. Despite wretched foul-shooting (they were 16-for-31 in the game), the Knicks squeezed out a 52–49 halftime lead. The last time New York visited Atlanta they ran the Hawks out of the gym during the third period. Wednesday it appeared that Richie Guerin's men planned to return the compliment. Stealing the ball almost at will from the sluggish New Yorkers, the Hawks ran to a 74–63 lead in the third quarter. However, Stallworth, Russell, and Riordan came off the bench at that point to relieve the shellshocked starters and pulled the Knicks back to within a point, 76–75, at quarter's end. But the revival was a false alarm. Paced throughout the game by Lou Hudson's 36 points and 27 by his running mate at guard, Walt Hazzard, the Hawks left the Knicks standing in the fourth quarter. The final score was 111–96, the Knicks worst defeat of the season. Walt Bellamy, playing his first game for Atlanta since being traded from Detroit, scored 10 points and had twelve rebounds in only 20 minutes. Later in the week, Bellamy scored 20 points and pulled down twenty rebounds. Maybe Richie Guerin can turn the puzzling center into a major asset, as he declared he could when the trade was announced.

The Knicks got well quickly against the Cincinnati Royals on Friday night. The Royals are really wallowing in woe with Oscar Robertston both unhappy and injured. Bob Wolff interviewed the star guard during halftime of the televised game and elicited some revealing comments. Oscar does not buy the Royals' contention that they can't afford his salary, nor will he wholeheartedly testify that Bob Cousy is not largely to blame for his and the team's troubles. Oscar made it very clear that he would not be playing for the Royals next season but that, as a professional who honors his contract, he would do his best to play for the remainder of this season. The groin injury, he assured Wolff, was genuine and not a convenient way to pull himself out of the lineup. With no more televised games scheduled this season from Cincinnati, the question becomes, "How will Bob Cousy get equal time?"

The Knicks, in any case, seemed to be attempting to

demonstrate what Oscar Robertson means to the Royals. A modest halftime advantage was expanded in the second half to an eventual 43-point victory, as the Knicks outscored the Royals 75–38 after the intermission. Everybody got into the act, with Donnie May pleasing the crowd with two long jumpers after his entry into the fray during the fourth quarter. May played his college ball at Dayton, not far from Cincinnati, and a contingent of his fans were at the game cheering loudly whenever he handled the ball. For their part, the Royals seemed disorganized and disheartened by the loss, playing out the string in a sluggish manner after the contest was decided in the third quarter.

On Saturday night the teams had a rematch in Madison Square Garden and the oddsmakers, keenly aware of the Knicks' showing on Friday night, made them a 15-point favorite. During the first half, it looked like a safe bet. At halftime the Knicks led 63–43. The Royals, however, refused to be humiliated two nights in a row. Connie Dierking and Johnny Green, two old pros, and Fred Foster, twenty-three years old, led the Royals to a second-half rally that made it close, 121–114 at the finish. The Cincinnati cause was aided by a slight muscle twinge sustained by Willis Reed that kept his playing time down to 32 minutes. He sat out almost the entire fourth quarter. Holzman pulled a change of tactics, installing Dave Stallworth at center for the last couple of mintues when Nate Bowman showed he was having difficulty handling the Royals' strength on the boards. Ultimately, it was Dave DeBusschere who assured the Knickerbocker victory, coming up with a key rebound and jump shot in the closing minutes to put the game out of reach.

Len Lewin writes in the *Post* today about "magic numbers," the sports terminology used in computing how close a team is to clinching a championship. Baltimore defeated second-place Milwaukee yesterday, so the Knicks' magic number against Milwaukee is down to 15—any combination of New York victories and Milwaukee defeats totaling fifteen will clinch the first New York Eastern Divsion championship since 1954. In more conventional language, the Knicks are 49–12, the Bucks are 41–19 and 7½ games behind. The Knicks have 21 games to play, the Bucks have 22.

I got to the game Saturday night to find two very strange people sitting in the seats next to us where Dan and his wife normally sit. The pair didn't look much like basketball fans. The gentleman punctuated the nods and grunts in his conversation with a constant gnawing on crackerjack and peanuts. The woman, whom I would estimate stood 5-foot-11 and scaled 185 pounds, kept up a nonstop chatter about her trips around the world, explaining in a thousand words or more why she *never* went to a World's Fair. As the layup drills and pregame shooting concluded and we were preparing to rise for the National Anthem, I said to my date that, more than anything else, I wished that Dan and his wife would walk in and we would find that these people were sitting in the seats by mistake.

Somewhere between "Oh say can you see" and "home of the brave," my prayer was answered. Holding his ticket stubs in an outstretched arm, Dan was leaning from the aisle, trying to get the interlopers out of his seats. The crackerjack-and-peanut gentleman took his hands out of the crackerjack box long enough to take Dan's stubs and study them, and then he and his wife/date/girlfriend (who knows?) vacated the seats, leaving a trail of litter. Dan said that he looked at the guy's tickets and they were for to-morrow night's hockey game. I found it hard to believe that two people could come to a hockey game and not know something was wrong when they saw twenty guys in sneakers shooting a round ball on layup lines, but that apparently was the case. Anyway, our intruders found two empty seats on the other side of the aisle and stayed to talk through the basketball game.

During the middle of the third quarter, a Garden usher

came up the aisle to the edge of our row and brusquely asked Dan whether he could see his ticket stubs. Finding they *were* for the seats Dan and his wife occupied, he flashed a disappointed smile and walked away. The real troublemakers, sitting across the aisle, were too engrossed in eating and talking to even notice the interruption we suffered.

The most encouraging thing about Knick play during the past week has been the apparent offensive resurgence of Dick Barnett. At the time of the season when old men are supposed to start fading away, Barnett seems to be getting stronger. With Walt Frazier a growing offensive threat and increasingly capable of piling up large point totals if left unguarded, the opposition has had less time to pay attention to the Knicks' old pro and he has responded by cashing in numerous assists from Frazier. More importantly, Barnett has been scoring and has done a lot of driving when he's been on the court with Mike Riordan, taking some of the defensive pressure off the Knicks' third guard. Earlier this season, Red Holzman expressed the opinion that Barnett has been one of the four top NBA guards of the last decade, with Cousy, Roberston, and West. Consistently, the Knick coach argued, he has gone out there and "done his thing." Apparently the days when he will no longer do so are not yet in sight.

This week is a light one for the Knicks. They begin a rest period today that will last until Wednesday, when they face the Celtics at the Garden. On Friday night they travel to Philadelphia and have a return match with the 76ers at the Garden on Saturday night. Then they get another couple of days off before they face Los Angeles at home. After a long road trip and a backbreaking schedule during the last winning streak, the days off must be welcome, if only to enjoy the anticipation of the pennant, which seems imminent.

RED HOLZMAN

Bob Wolff had suggested that I could expedite the process of interviewing the Knicks by visiting one of their practice sessions. Although I had made it clear time and time again to the p.r. department that I was available to interview or make interview appointments at any time, neither Blauschild nor Wergeles had ever made the suggestion.

The Knicks practice at the Lost Battalion Hall on Queens Boulevard. Like a typical Manhattanite, I am lost when I wander out of my island borough, so I trusted a veteran cabdriver to lead me. He needed directions, but we finally found the place and I walked in—as Blauschild suggested I do after I had posed the idea to him—near the end of practice at eleven-forty-five.

By the time I got there, the only starter in sight was Dave DeBusschere. Cazzie Russell, Nate Bowman, Dave Stallworth, Donnie May, and Bill Hosket were all shooting. Johnny Warren's shots drew the most attention of the orderly crowd of about twenty-five young men, most of them Negro, watching the practice. Off in a corner, practicing pretty much by himself, was Phil Jackson.

It took me a moment or two to become oriented to the fact that the players were just engaging in some free shooting practice and that the organized session must have concluded. As I became aware of that, two men who had been standing under a basket and watching the session walked toward me. I realized that I was about to meet Red Holzman, the Knick coach, and trainer Danny Whelan.

I followed Holzman and Whelan to a small locker room that serves as Holzman's office, asking the Knick coach if an interview could be set up with him. He wryly questioned my credentials and asked where I had been, showing up to do a book with the season nearly over. I explained the nature of the book and how I had been attempting to interview him and the Knick players since the season began. His disbelief must have resulted from the unending stream of journalists and authors he has faced this season. The strength of their numbers might lead him to think that the Knick publicity office had done an excellent job of steering writers straight to the interview.

I explained to Holzman, as he lit up a cigar, that I was doing the book primarily from the point of view of the fan, and for openers I asked him whether he felt he could have done what he did with the Knicks in a city where the fans were less knowledgeable.

Through a thin trail of exhaled smoke the coach replied, "How should I know? I've never tried it anyplace but here."

I persisted. Did he think that the knowledgeability of the fans made it easier to coach, to get players to do things other than score?

"No."

I must admit I was rattled. I thought I had asked pretty sensible questions, particularly considering the pleasure Donnie May had expressed about being cheered for good deeds other than putting the ball through the hoop. Holzman seemed to sense my discomfort and began to open up. He started to answer the questions more openly and, in doing so, revealed as much about his own temperament as he did about his feelings about the game.

Did he think that fans overcomplicated the game?

"Well, I don't think that basketball is as complex as some fans and writers think it is," he said. "There really isn't anything new in basketball, nothing new with what we're doing this year."

Was it really that simple? I wondered. How about in drafting players? Weren't there secrets?

"No," he said. "We just draft the best player available, regardless of position. And there are no scerets. The pros know who the best players coming up are." He indicated that drafting regardless of position had helped the Knicks in putting together their current crop of ballplayers.

Did he frequently find it necessary to make adjustments at halftime?

"It's always necessary. Something happens in every basketball game that you didn't anticipate. Sometimes you're even stymied, unable to put your finger on what is going wrong. We just do the best we can."

I asked Holzman if the players were aware of the point spreads. He seemed to be insulted by the question, but I continued, explaining that a Madison Square Garden fan existed in a climate of gambling. During the time I was interviewing Holzman, players had been drifting into the locker room to pick up their valuables. At the time of this question, Dave DeBusschere was passing through and seemed to wear a look of distinct displeasure.

"No," Holzman said. "I have never heard of any gambling by the players, or interest in it, and I don't want to degrade myself by discussing it."

I went on and asked why Cincinnati had given the Knicks so much trouble earlier this year. Was Oscar Robertson the main reason?

"Without a doubt, Oscar. He controls the game—but he controls it so *well*. But they have a lot of good players on the Royals. They nearly won that game from us on Saturday night without Oscar. He's not the only player on the team." But Holzman admitted that Robertson was probably the primary reason for the Royals' early-season success against the Knicks.

By this time, Holzman had apparently decided that I was okay to talk to, so he surprised me by asking me some questions. "What about your hair? Are you considered attractive in your age group?"

Now, how the hell do you answer a question like that?

I told him, for whatever help it was, that my girlfriend had cut it.

"Yeah, my daughter likes it on guys too. Isn't that something, Dan?" Whelan nodded. "You know," said Red, "these kids today are really something."

Whelan and Holzman then began a discussion about my generation, evaluating the political attitudes and mores in a most complimentary fashion. Whelan commented that their generation was one of followers, ours was one of leaders.

Holzman went on, talking about changes that politicians had been forced to make because of the pressure of young people. He asked me how old I was.

"Twenty-three," I answered, adding five months to inflate the answer.

"Look at that, Dan. Young enough to be one of mine and writing this book."

This again led to a discussion of youth, during which Holzman commented that he agreed with the young most of the time, except on the question of drugs. He thought he never could be persuaded on that. "You know," he said, "you and I ought to do a book together. One of us from each generation."

I said it sounded like a good idea to me.

"Our generation didn't have time for all these things, you know. We had to worry about when we'd be eating—we just supplied our own entertainment. We didn't have the opportunity that you kids have, and we didn't do as much."

By this time the pile of wallets and wristwatches on the table had vanished and it was clear that the practice was all over, the players gone home. I was wondering if I should leave and let Holzman and Whelan go home.

But then Red started the conversation again. "How am I going to know if you're legit?" He and Whelan talked about a fan in San Francisco who had posed as an author so he could talk to the players.

I told Holzman that Blauschild would vouch for me. "But how does *he* know?"

Holzman smiled when I told him the Knick office had gotten a letter from Prentice-Hall before the season started. "Well, okay, then. You know, I like you—you're a good boy. I wouldn't mind having you for a son of mine, and I wouldn't want to find out that you're a phoney." His smile continued as the words ceased, then he began again. "And don't worry about coming in to the practices and getting your interviews. We'll let you know if you're bothering us, nicely."

Holzman seems more multidimensional than Donnie May or Darrall Imhoff, my previous introductions to the mind of the athlete. Red has made a career out of playing, coaching, and scouting basketball, but he has made his lifetime out of far more pieces. He talked about his reading and how it had shifted from fiction to history. He talked briefly about politics, at length about the generation gap. He admits that he spends as little of his spare time as possible on basketball. He obviously enjoys the game, but he treats it as his profession, not his life.

Red seems not to buy many of the shibboleths about professional athletics. His attitude seems to be that these ballplayers are professionals and can be expected to do their job—playing ball, talking to reporters—in a professional manner without undue regard to outside pressures. He didn't think that the fans' razzing affected Howard Komives or the team unduly when he played in New York. "These guys are professionals." He didn't think that an interview prior to a game should affect the way the Knicks performed on the court. "These guys are professionals." He finds no problem maintaining morale with a star-studded bench. "These guys are professionals. They are expected to be able to do their job when they are needed." Period. *These guys are professionals.* And so is Holzman.

In all the portrayals of Holzman that have appeared in

the local press since the rapid rise of the team, this point has never been underscored. His wry humor and ability to disarm an interviewer without seemingly trying have been discussed. His unworrying attitude—"Never worry about anything you can't do anything about"—is a famous component of his character. To me, however, these qualities seemed dwarfed by his professionalism. Holzman is a complete human being with a professional specialty. He does not need to glorify or complicate his specialty to underscore his professionalism. His credentials are in the league standings for anybody who wants to see them. He has succeeded where others failed. He does his job well and he expects the same of those who work for him.

The local press has indicated this only by what is *not* reported about the Knicks, because it doesn't happen. Holzman does not complain about officiating, which is acknowledged to be at one of its lowest ebbs since the dawn of the NBA. He does not make excuses for losses or justify strategic maneuvers. He does his job, oblivious to the external pressures of hundreds of thousands of vocal fans who take more interest in the Knicks than most stockholders do in a company they own a piece of. "These guys are professionals."

JOHNNY WARREN

Having been sidetracked from speaking to any ballplayers when I first went to a Knick practice by the amiable and loquacious Mr. Holzman, I made a reasonably determined effort to avoid him the following day and pursued the ballplayers. Their answers to my request for an interview were as diverse as their basketball talent: Dick Barnett was evasive, promising nothing, answering no questions, opening no doors; Dave Stallworth begged off politely but suggested that in a week or two his schedule might have lightened to the point where he would have time; Mike Riordan wondered if I might be making any of the road trips with the team, since that would be the most convenient time for him; Willis Reed agreed to be interviewed but asked that either Blauschild or Wergeles set the time to fit in with his schedule.

Johnny Warren, the Knicks' only rookie, was the easiest to pin down. He quickly agreed to meet me the next night at the Garden before the Celtic game. In the interests of having plenty of time for the interview and allowing him to be ready for the game, we agreed to meet at five o'clock.

I arrived at the Garden half-an-hour early, hoping to find one or two more Knicks on the scene before the game so that I could make more interview appointments. None of the pros were around, but the St. Peter's basketball team was holding a practice in preparation for their game the following night. Warren arrived almost on the dot of five, and as we shook hands he said, "I was afraid you might have gone. The cat downstairs said you walked in two hours ago."

We sat down in the loge seats overlooking the St. Peter's practice to have our conversation. Warren asked me about the book and seemed pleased to hear that there would be a chapter entitled "Johnny Warren."

I asked him what has been the toughest part of the transition from collegiate forward to professional guard. "Ballhandling and defense, I guess," he said. "I was lucky because we played good 'd' at St. John's, but some of the players in this league are something else. You take a guy like Dave Bing, 6-foot-3, and with his speed and his moves you just hope you can stay with him. All those moves!"

Warren's admiration for Bing should not indicate that he has any doubts about his own ability. "I thought I'd play more this year, you know. My biggest problem is to keep my confidence up. I know I can do the job."

With an expansion draft coming up after the season, would he be doing the job in New York?

"I'd like to stay here and play here. But there's good and bad to it either way because I'd like to play more. We don't talk about it much—the expansion—but I guess it's on our minds. Right now we're more worried about winning the championship."

Were the pros as tough as he had expected?

"No, nothing surprised me very much. I thought the travel would be tougher than it is, except for one trip we made starting after a Christmas game here. That was amazing—Los Angeles on Friday night, Vancouver on Saturday night, Phoenix on Sunday night, and then we had an afternoon game here on Tuesday. I don't know how the guys that are playing all the time did it. I was tired just from the traveling."

What about the contact in pro ball, often mentioned as the difference bewteen college and pro ranks?

"No, again not as tough as I expected. You know, with all I heard I thought it was going to be all elbows and rough stuff up here, but it isn't so bad. Really isn't."

I asked Warren whether the rookies in the league talked to each other much, whether there was any sort of "Rookie's Union."

"Certainly is. I talk to a lot of them: Lucius Allen of Seattle, Rackley at Cincinnati, McCarter and Garrett of L.A. We talk about playing time. That's the big thing. Playing Time. You know, that's why that thing with Mc-Carter makes me wonder."

We discussed the problems rookie Willie McCarter had in L.A. when he refused to enter a ballgame late in the fourth quarter to play out the remaining moments when the issue was decided. I told Warren I thought I could understand his feelings, going in with 2 minutes remaining.

"Two minutes?" he said. "Is that all it was. Maybe that's

it. I've heard it was 6 minutes. That's a lot of playing time, 6 minutes. I could score 12 points in 6 minutes." He chuckled.

I asked Warren about when he first came to Knick camp. He must have been pretty much alone. Was there any veteran who was easiest to talk to?

"Willis." There was no hesitation. "I think Willis is the man everybody talks to on this team. He's the captain, the big man."

Warren claimed not to notice the fans in other cities. To him it seemed that opposition fans were simply opposition fans. Concerning the local spectators, he had more to say. "The fans here are the greatest, Absolutely unbelievable. Now, you take last Saturday night after we had beaten Cincinnati by 43 the night before and there was still a full house here on Saturday. Nineteen-five, nineteen-five almost every night. And the way they're always behind you, sticking around to watch everybody play. They're just the greatest."

I asked Warren why some great collegiate ballplayers failed to make it in the pros. I suggested Barry Kramer and Dave Schellhase, ex-stalwarts of NYU and Purdue, respectively, who had flopped in the NBA.

"That is a good question. I really don't know." Later on, however, he himself offered a clue when he talked about Dick Garrett and Willie McCarter of the Lakers. "I think Garrett had an edge there because he played with Southern Illinois, where Walt played, and they really teach you defense there. You know, Garrett had less to learn about defense up here."

Was Lew Alcindor part of the Rookie's Union?

"No, I don't think so anymore. Lew's had so much playing time, he's really a veteran. Did you see in the paper where Costello plans to play him 48 minutes a game for the rest of the season?"

I suggested that the longer pro game and pro season should start wearing down a rookie.

Warren nodded. "I'll be happy when the season's over," he said. "It's not really that I'm tired of it, but I'll be glad when it's over."

I asked him how he felt about the Knicks' chances before the season started. Had he envisioned anything like the success they've been enjoying?

"No," he said. "I thought we'd really have a battle. I never thought we'd be what we are—what? about 35 games over .500. But then, earlier in the season, when we were on the streak, I thought we'd never lose again. 'Ain't nobody gonna beat us.'"

What happened to the team after the eighteen-game streak?

"Just a slump, man, just a slump. I guess it happens to every team."

Johnny Warren is a man in a very ticklish position. He chose to go with the Knicks in the NBA instead of the Nets in the ABA because he felt he could do the job in the tougher league. The choice was made easier for him because, either way, he got to play in New York, the scene of his collegiate success and where he was already known and appreciated by the fans. As the 1969–70 season draws to a close, he has participated on a first-place squad, but his own ability is still in doubt. The season has not proved that he won't be a good pro, but neither has it proved that he will. His concern about playing time is revealing—only by getting more of it will he be able to answer the question. Now he faces the next season with little proven, and at least a 50–50 chance that he's going to move to an expansion franchise. I asked him about the reserve clause in an athlete's contract that prohibits him from selling his services on the free market.

"No, I don't get upset about that. I think that's just part of the profession, an occupational hazard."

The key to the Knicks' success: Willis Reed goes over three Warrior players to score. UPI

A calm Mr. Holzman at practice. UPI

A not-so-calm Mr. Holzman at a game. UPI

Dick Barnett, going for the basket. UPI

Cazzie Russell, going for the basket. UPI

Walt Frazier, one lay-up style. UPI

Mike Riordan, another lay-up style. UPI

Willis Reed, his own lay-up style. UPI

Broken nose or no, De-Busschere is under the boards. UPI

"The Workhorse of the Knicks," De Busschere. UPI

The Knicks on defense:
Willis Reed leads the way.
UPI

The Knicks on defense:
The Celtics lose the ball.
UPI

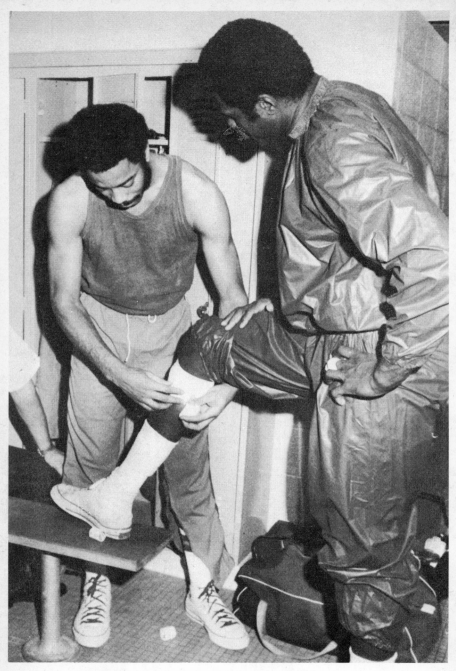

When Willis is hurting, everybody is ready to help. UPI

It would be unfortunate for Johnny Warren if he had to go, because he really likes it with the Knicks, even without a lot of playing time. Aside from his appreciation of the home-town fans, he likes Coach Holzman—"He has *all* my respect." He is aware that Dick Barnett is thirty-three years old and cannot be a regular for too many more years. He has watched Mike Riordan emerge as a third guard who gets a lot of "playing time," a lot of points, a lot of press attention, and a lot of deserved credit for the Knicker-bockers' success.

Johnny Warren is, perhaps, the most enigmatic of all the Knickerbockers. His collegiate success and self-confidence are beyond question, but little else is. This is a situation that is certainly not his fault. In many seasons past, when the Knicks were not a first-place team, his arrival would have been heralded and he would have been thrown into the breech to succeed or fail. Even having achieved a select spot, one of twelve men who collectively do what they do better than any other twelve men in the world, he has not really had the opportunity to achieve personal success or suffer personal failure.

FEBRUARY 17

If you remember the thrilling adventures of the New York Knickerbockers from last week, you will recall that they lost on Wednesday, won a crusher on Friday, and then beat the team that they had crushed by a slender margin on Satur-day. Would you believe that the same thing happened again this past week?

I had noticed that Bill Bradley and Walt Frazier were absent from the practice I attended on Tuesday afternoon. As it turned out, neither played in the game against Boston on Wednesday night. Bradley's ankle, which had sidelined him briefly almost ten days ago, was hurting again, so he also missed the games Friday and Saturday night. Frazier simply had a touch of the flu and was too weak to play against the Celtics.

Things started out for the Knicks as if the absence of their two stars wouldn't matter. A quick start and early big bulge against the Celtics was wasted, however, as the defending NBA champs fought back to take a 55–48 lead at halftime. In the third quarter, Willis Reed came on with a flurry of baskets—he finished with 40 points—bringing the Knicks to within one point at 76–75. The rally continued into the fourth quarter before John Havlicek, on whom the Celtics have relied for years, and Jo-Jo White, on whom they must now increasingly rely, led Boston back again. A jumper by Reed gave the Knicks a 2-point lead with 10 seconds to go, but White saved a busted play (the ball was supposed to go to Havlicek) to score for the Celtics and send the game into overtime.

The Knickerbockers were overmatched in the extra session. With Dave DeBusschere having fouled out, Reed terribly tired, and Bradley and Frazier not in the Garden, they finally succumbed to their thirteenth defeat of the year—their third at the hands of the Celtics.

On Friday the Knicks made the short hop to Philadelphia to play the 76ers in the first of a home-and-home series. The 76ers will always remember that the game was on Friday the thirteenth, since the Knicks won, 151–106. The issue was never in doubt, as the Knicks led by as much as 40 in the second quarter on their way to an 80–46 halftime lead. Cazzie Russell and Dick Barnett led the scoring: Caz scored 35 points in three quarters, hitting 14-for-21 from the floor, and Barnett hit on 10-of-11. Everybody got into the act before the debacle was completed. The simplest explanation of this game is that everything went right for the Knicks and everything went wrong for Philadelphia. The only hopeful quote printed in the next day's papers from the 76er standpoint was from Darrall Imhoff—he promised that the same thing would not happen on Saturday night at the Garden.

Yet, for a while it seemed that it would. The Knicks again jumped quickly from the gun, but determined Philadelphia play and New York foul trouble combined to turn the tide to the 76ers in the second half. With more than half of the fourth quarter gone, a spurt carried Philly to a 105–101 lead. From that point, the momentum switched for a couple of minutes and the Knicks ran off 9-straight points, only to have Philadelphia tie the game at 110. Ultimately, the Knicks turned to foul-saddled Dave DeBusschere to pull them out of the hole. Dave brought five personals off the bench with him to play the closing minutes, but avoided his sixth foul and disqualification while hitting the key jump shot and pulling down the key rebound to assure the Knick victory. Even with DeBusschere's heroics, overtime seemed possible when Frazier missed 2 out of 3 foul shots with 3 seconds left, giving Philadelphia the ball under the Knick basket and needing only 2 points to tie. But the unfortunate 76ers had no times-out remaining, and a hurried out-of-bounds pass from Darrall Imhoff to Hal Greer went astray. Willis Reed picked up the loose ball and held on as the clock ran out.

The game against the 76ers on Saturday night was particularly noteworthy for two reasons. The first was the officiating, which was dreadful. There seems to be general agreement that it has deteriorated sadly this year. The explanation most frequently offered for this, by Darrall Imhoff among others, is that expansion and the jumping of four qualified officials to the ABA has watered down the talent and experience among referees. The officials on Saturday night seemed confused, often out of position, and indecisive. The most blatant "missed call" of the night came as the buzzer sounded for the end of the first half and a shot that Walt Frazier had launched from the far frontiers of the Knick backcourt dropped through the hoop. The refs ruled "no goal," indicating that the shot had been taken after the buzzer. This was clearly *not* the case, the ball being in the air and fully halfway to the basket when the buzzer sounded. What probably happened was that the referees, little expecting a shot to go in from that distance, paid little attention to the relative timing of Frazier's release and the buzzer. In any case, the error cost the Knicks 2 points that very nearly were the difference between a victory and a defeat.

The second thing that makes the Philadelphia game noteworthy is couched in a larger question—should Cazzie Russell be playing regularly? Since he has replaced Bradley in the starting lineup—albeit temporarily—Cazzie has averaged over 20 points per game. His shooting has been explosive, his passing has been good, his rebounding improving. The suggestion that Cazzie continue to start after Bradley's recovery is complete—probably this Saturday—has been broached in the stands and in the press.

I do not agree. The Philadelphia game and the relative success that Cazzie and Donnie May had guarding Jim Washington dramatize the reason why I do not agree. Cazzie Russell still can not play adequate defense in the NBA. Washington scored 22 points in Saturday night's game, and as I remember, every one of them was off Cazzie. During one stretch of the second half, about 6 minutes long, while May was guarding Washington, the Philadelphia forward managed to get the ball only twice: once on a defensive rebound after a missed Knick foul shot, and once in the backcourt when he helped to break a Knick press. Needless to say, Washington failed to score off May. In the meantime, May had time to help out his teammates enough that he drew a couple of personal fouls, sending other 76ers to the line.

May is not one of the top defensive forwards in basketball, primarily because of the height disadvantage he has playing forward at 6-foot-4. However, his adequate defensive skills combined with his concentration and defensive effort were enough to stop Washington when Cazzie could not. This is not to indicate that Cazzie Russell is not an important part of the team, nor that he would not consistently score more points than either May or Bradley. But his defensive ability, particularly compared with the outstanding job Bradley is capable of doing against forwards of all sizes, make it to the Knicks' advantage to continue using Cazzie as an explosive sixth man.

I was to make the trip to Philadelphia last Friday with the Knicks, but at the last minute the publicity office announced a problem in transporting me. I am assured by Bob Wolff, whose concern led him to inquire, that no ill will was intended by the Knick publicity people, despite my feelings to the contrary. Here are the facts.

Wolff and I had agreed when I interviewed him two weeks ago that it would be a good idea for me to make the Philadelphia trip. He told me that I should inform Blauschild so that he could provide the necessary arrangements. I assumed—and I think Wolff assumed at that time—that Blauschild would speak to Philadelphia publicist Bob Vetrone about press credentials for me and arrange for me to be included in the car pool of writers traveling to Philadelphia.

I told Blauschild about the trip immediately after my conversation with Wolff and agreed to call back the following week for details. When I called him early last week, he told me that he wasn't sure he could provide a ride and would not know until Friday morning, the day of the game. He then asked me whether I had called Vetrone in Philadelphia to let him know I was coming. I said no and added that I had assumed Blauschild would be in touch with

Vetrone and would give him a complete list of those who needed accreditation and press seats. Blauschild, reluctantly I thought, agreed to speak to Vetrone, and I, reluctantly I know, agreed to wait until Friday morning to find out about a ride.

When I called on Friday morning I was put off by a secretary, who told me that Blauschild wouldn't be in the office until about one. When I explained the nature of the problem, she told me not to worry, since nobody would leave before three-thirty, but suggested that I try to get the Knick official about twelve-thirty, in case he got in early. I reached him at the earlier time to find out there would be no ride. The explanation I got was that the writers were going down at three-thirty and then going out to dinner. "You don't want to go down that early," he suggested, carefully omitting issuing a dinner invitation to join them.

"I really don't mind," I said, even though I did. I figured I had little choice. I didn't know how little choice.

"What are you going to do down there?" Blauschild asked me. "You don't have any idea where the Spectrum is. It's in the middle of nowhere."

"I'll find something."

"Oh, yeah. But we can't offer you a ride back."

Stunned, I wondered why he waited to tell me that. "Why?"

"Well, Phil Pepe of the *News* and I are coming back in my car and we're just going straight home. We live in Jersey. The other car is going to the Island but it'll be full, since there will only be two of us in my car. I really think it would easier for you to check on your own arrangements."

Somewhat at a loss, I called Wolff. He agreed that it made little sense for me to make the trip under the circumstances (among them that the game was being televised). With the extent of doubt about the ride, I was concerned about what press status I would have when I got to Philadelphia. I certainly did not want to go down there alone to be a spectator when I could much more comfortably be one, with company, in my own living room.

Wolff promised to check into things and call me back this morning. Blauschild, it seems, explained that he couldn't spend much time helping anybody but the regular writers with their problems—getting into games, lining up interviews—and other writers had pretty much to shift for themselves. He assured Wolff that no personal slight was intended. Wolff suggested that I be more aggressive on my own in making appointments with the ballplayers. I promised to start doing so, but I reminded Wolff that Willis Reed had asked that Wergeles make my appointments for him. Could I still trust the office to do that?

Wolff assured me that I could and told me to let him know if I ran into any more insurmountable difficulty. I thanked him. I must admit I am somewhat flabbergasted at the interest Wolff has taken in the book and the amount of assistance he has offered. His explanation for the Knick office's lack of interest in assisting me was that they had little to gain. By that reasoning, Wolff also has nothing to gain, so I must assume he is helping me because he happens to be one hell of a nice guy. In any case, I feel that my initial opinion of him, dating from the first time I approached him about an interview, has been strongly buttressed. Finding that there are still people at the top of their profession who are concerned about people who are not is a comforting discovery. This alone is probably enough to make writing this book worthwhile.

On Bob Wolff's advice, I stopped in at the office today and Wergeles promised an interview with Reed next Tuesday. It is difficult to discern these things precisely, but I felt a more cooperative attitude in the publicity office today, perhaps attributable to the words Wolff spoke to Blauschild in my behalf.

In fairness to all concerned, it should be made clear that Wolff has pulled no strings, nor has he attempted to circumvent or help me circumvent the commandos who guard the players from interviewers' intrusions. On the other hand, his expertise and advice have been made constantly available to me and he has not been afraid to speak up in my behalf. When I interviewed Wolff, he talked with great pride of the things people with whom he had been associated from time to time had done. His eagerness to help shove somebody down the road to success is matched only by his concern that he not trespass on the territory of others in so doing. It would be an unwarranted disservice to Bob Wolff if I were to create the impression that he pulled rank or led an end sweep around Blauschild and Wergeles in any way. What can be stated fairly, however, is that the best p.r. man for the Garden and for the Knicks I've encountered has been Bob Wolff.

WILLIS REED

The strength of the Knick bench this year has raised the issue of which starter would be the most difficult to replace. I must concur with the almost-unanimous opinion in the press that it would be Willis Reed—captain, center, leading scorer and rebounder. No insult is intended here to Nate Bowman, Bill Hosket, and Dave Stallworth, who have played center at times throughout the season. But Reed is the bulwark, and with Thurmond and Chamberlain injured and Alcindor still a rookie, Willis is undoubtedly the top center in the NBA.

Willis is the team leader by acclamation of his teammates, not merely by appointment of management. His play on the court reflects this. He is quiet and strong, often the man looked to for a key basket, often the man who picks up driving opponents who have skirted the perimeter of the Knick defense, always the smart ballplayer who can be trusted not to lose his head in the closing stages of a tight game. Willis has been quoted as saying that the ball belongs to Frazier and that only when Walt wants to let go do the other players get to handle it. He leaves unsaid the fact that Willis Reed is the man who gets Walt Frazier the ball, off the boards and by blocking shots.

Bob Wolff suggested that Willis was cooperative and friendly, a good man to approach for an interview. I spoke to him in the locker room of Lost Battalion after a practice and he readily agreed to meet with me, but asked that I have the Knick office set the time and place. I spoke to Jim Wergeles the next day and he set a date a week away, for five-thirty in the afternoon before a ballgame with Phoenix. The meeting place was a sandwich shop that Willis owns a piece of, Willis Reed's Beef and Bun.

I called the Knick office the day of the interview to confirm it and was told that there was somebody else scheduled for the same time, but Wergeles was "sure you could do it together." I balked at this and wondered whether another time would be more convenient. I was angry at facing yet another roadblock placed by the publicity office. Wergeles was sure there would be adequate time for both of us, despite the fact that Willis had a ball game at seven-thirty and, according to what I understood from Danny Whelan, would be expected in the locker room by six or so.

I got to Beef and Bun on the dot of five-thirty, but Willis didn't get there until five-fifty. This was not his fault—he had to go to the doctor's to have a contused finger checked. Meanwhile, the other interviewer apparently got rattled by the delay and was not present when Willis walked in.

I suggested to Willis that if time was too short for him now we could do the interview another time. He said there was no problem—he had to have a bite to eat in any case.

103

We sat down at the counter, where I had already ordered my pregame fare, to talk.

I told Willis that John Warren had said that he was the "man to talk to" for all the ballplayers on the team. He took the compliment in stride, but not in an arrogant way. It was clear that had any other player been accorded that role it would have surprised him.

"Tom Gola was the man like that when I first came up," said Willis. (Gola was a guard in the NBA for over a decade, spending the last few years of his career with the Knicks.) "I guess it's me for a variety of reasons now. First, I've been with this club longer than anybody else. Secondly, I'm the captain."

I asked Willis whether he had any trouble getting "up" for games. This is a common topic of conversation in the press. It is said that Bill Russell threw up in the locker room before crucial games when he played with the Celtics, and athletes making the transition from thirty college games to ninety pro games (including exhibitions) in their rookie years are faced with a psychological adjustment, not just a physical one.

"It's a team thing," Willis said. "I know that some ballgames are more important than others. Like when we're playing Milwaukee or Baltimore, they could pick up a full game in the standings by beating us. I am aware of the fact that it's different when we're playing, say, Seattle."

Isn't there a personal factor, I wondered, such as that Alcindor and Unseld play for Milwaukee and Baltimore, and that Willis knows he will personally have a tough opponent?

"No, there's none of that, really. What I'm worried about is the team. I scored 40 points recently and we lost. What good is that? I'd much rather score 20 and have us win. I know I've got a job to do, no matter who we play, if we're going to win. When everybody does his job, we do win."

104

Is there a great variation between playing in one city or another on the road?

"Yes, definitely. The fans you really don't want to play for are in Philly and Boston. You know, they're impolite, unappreciative."

It had occurred to me that a parallel was developing between Willis Reed and Bill Russell. Russell was the key man for the Celtics during an unprecedented reign of eleven championships in thirteen years. It looks like the Knicks may be beginning a dynasty of their own, although it is impossible to project success comparable to Boston's in length. However, Willis's status as the indispensable man is similar. I asked him how much longer he planned to play.

"Well, I hope I could play about six more years."

Do you think you would ever want to coach?

"No, man, that doesn't interest me at all. It's just not my idea of a life."

What was the main reason for the Knicks' improvement this year? Could it be traced to any single ballplayer, like Dave DeBusschere?

"There are twelve reasons for it. Every ballplayer on this team is responsible for it. There's no selfishness, this is a twelve-man team."

A question that nobody has been able to answer to my satisfaction is why some real good college ballplayers fail to make it in the pros. Johnny Warren admitted being stumped by it, and Red Holzman said he couldn't begin to answer it. Willis had thoughts on the matter.

"I think the big thing is when a ballplayer reaches this full potentiality," Willis said. "Some guys reach the top when they're still in college and they don't keep improving after that. Other guys don't reach their full potentiality until they're in the pros."

We discussed Mike Riordan, who was never a star at Providence but who has come on like gangbusters with the

Knicks. "The game's tougher up here and you got to improve. In college, you might play against one All-American in a season, play against him for two games. *Everybody* up here is All-American, you know. You have to keep improving."

During our conversation, Willis excused himself several times as he turned to talk to fans who came over and asked for autographs. He turned down no requests and had a few kind words for everybody who spoke with him. On top of that, he remembered the names of some of the younger kids who had obviously discovered earlier in the season that Willis grabbed a bite at his place before every game. Many celebrities are gracious about signing autographs, but I had never seen anybody as sincerely friendly about it as Willis Reed.

I asked him who he felt the underrated players in the NBA were.

"There's lots of them, some on every club. With us I'd say it's Dick Barnett. You know, they all talk about a Walt Frazier, a Willis Reed, a Dave DeBusschere, but Barnett is doing the job night after night. There's many other guys, like Bill Bridges in Atlanta and Darrall Imhoff in Philadelphia. They don't get the recognition they deserve."

I asked Willis about his outside interests, besides the Beef and Bun.

"Well, I've got the summer camp. I really like kids. And I'm planning to open up a clothing store near Grambling. I think they still know who I am down there—they haven't had a lot of pro-basketball players. It's more of a football school."

Then I asked whether there was a big increase in the demands on his time this year.

"Well, you're here. That indicates something," he answered, laughing. "Really, would you be here if we were in the same position as, say, Seattle?"

106

I told him that I had decided to do the book *before* the season started.

"Still, man, you could tell by the way we finished last year that we were going to have something, couldn't you? No, I don't mind, as long as we win that championship."

By this time the deep bowl of fruit that had been in front of Willis had nearly disappeared, so I supposed he was about ready to cross the street for the Garden. "Well, thanks an awful lot," I said. "I've really enjoyed talking to you. You've been very helpful."

Willis looked surprised. He didn't realize that we were finished. "Oh? Okay. Certainly glad I could help."

Willis comes across personally in much the same way that he does on the court. He is intimidatingly strong, but he punctuates his strength with such grace that one can easily forget the presence of that imposing brute force of which he is capable. In a ballgame, Willis will frequently take the longer route to the basket, outfinessing his opponent and going around him. On the other hand, he leaves no question that he could take a more direct route to the hoop if he were so inclined, regardless of what roadblocks might be placed in his way.

So with the interview. Upon occasion, such as when he is asked about coaching, he chooses a direct route—"not my idea of a life." The ball has been jammed through the hoop —you understand exactly what he means. Most of the time, however, he accomplishes his verbal points with finesse, such as by kidding me about asking about the Knicks' increased publicity by pointing out that I was part of the increase.

Willis Reed is totally on top of the situation the great majority of the time, on the floor and off it. He says he is glad to be playing in New York—"I always said that, even when I was playing forward." He has commanded respect from his teammates and expanded his interests in New York. No mean trick for a man of rural Southern upbringing in the most complex and fast-paced city in the country.

MARCH 8—Boston Garden

I decided to skip the March 8 afternoon game the Knicks had with Philadelphia in favor of a trip to Boston to see the Milwaukee Bucks play the Celtics. There were several reasons:

I hoped, through Kenny Heitz, to get a hold of Lew Alcindor and interview him. Heitz was a teammate of Lew's for four years at UCLA and is now at Harvard Law School.

The Knicks game was scheduled for a national ABC telecast in the afternoon and the Celtic game was scheduled for the evening, so I knew I wouldn't really "miss" the Knick game.

I wanted to find out how the experience of watching pro basketball in Boston differed from that in New York.

Reaching Alcindor turned out to be impossible. Apparently, the Bucks had always stayed at a particular motel in Cambridge near Logan Airport and the Boston Garden, but they had switched accommodations on this trip and Kenny and I couldn't find them. So much for a possible interview.

The Knick game was a disaster. After having squeezed by the 76ers the night before in Philadelphia, the Knicks couldn't stop Billy Cunningham from taking them apart in the Garden. Folks all over the country got to see the 76ers' star forward score 39 points and corral about twenty rebounds in leading his team to victory. Both Willis Reed and Dave DeBusschere had three fouls in the first quarter. Dave Stallworth was a miracle man coming off the bench in the second quarter, but the locals couldn't pull themselves together in the second half.

But the trip to Boston Garden made it all worthwhile.

108

Alcindor and John Havlicek of the Celtics locked up in a scoring duel that Alcindor, and the Bucks, finally won, 138–134. Lew gracefully poured through 44 points, 20 of them coming on foul shots, and drew six disqualifying fouls from both Henry Finkel and Rich Johnson and five from third-string center Jim "Bad News" Barnes. Havlicek was his usual perpetual-motion self, driving for most of his 43 points.

Boston Garden sits above North Station as Madison Square Garden is built above Penn Station. It would be possible to go from one to the other without ever stepping outside by catching a Penn Central train from North Station to Grand Central and heading straight to the subway and coming up directly into Madison Square Garden. More interesting than that to me was how close the Boston Garden is to Logan Airport—no more than ten minutes away. I had always pitied the Celtics for having to play a night game in New York followed by a day game in Boston, but this is probably easier on them than it is for many New York players to go home and come back to Madison Square Garden the following day.

The entrances from North Station to the Boston Garden are not as clearly marked as they are in New York, the first indication that one will not encounter the neon-lighted beauty that characterizes Madison Square Garden. Around dark ramps and passageways that feel like the entrance to elevated catacombs, you walk until you come to the Boston Garden lobby.

Finding your seats from the lobby is not the easy proposition it is in New York. Fewer signs direct you, fewer ushers help you. On the assumption that my balcony tickets required me to walk upstairs, I finally found my way to the level my seats called for. Finding the proper section was another problem entirely. It developed that I walked the entire circumference of the balcony before coming upon the right section. The hallways surrounding the level were dark and dismal. I don't think I'd like to walk them alone.

On our way around I saw seats from which only the smallest corner of the court could be seen, partly because of buttresses and partly because of the overhang of the steep second balcony above us. While I am sure that the Celtics do not sell these seats, I wondered how primitive stadium architecture must have been thirty or forty years ago to have allowed them to be built.

Once settled in my seat, I decided to hunt for a program. I have often wished not to be so besieged as I am in New York by vendors hawking programs, yearbooks, posters, and other nonedible garbage. After my trip to Boston, however, I must grudgingly admit that they perform a service. The concession stand had no programs. I wondered whether there were any sold here at all and was told they were available in the lobby. But I was not going to walk back down there to get one. I really wondered whether I'd be able to find my way back.

The Boston Garden crowd is distinctly different from the New York. The percentage of men in the total crowd is definitely higher. I would guess that 30 percent of the New York crowd is female; in Boston the percentage may be a third of that. Perhaps as a result of this, the men are considerably less well-dressed in Boston. Most of the Knick fans *look* like businessmen. Jackets and ties are the rule rather than the exception, although I seldom wear either and am not made to feel uncomfortable or underdressed. In Boston I might think the person that wears a jacket and tie would be uncomfortable for being *over*dressed. The tenor of the crowd is proportionately rougher. Personal vindictive remarks against members of the opposition and of the home team are heard frequently. In New York they are heard less frequently and almost *never* shouted out. Rather, distasteful remarks are made for the ears of immediately surrounding fans, not intended for the players on the court.

110

On the other hand, fans are not so close to the action in New York. My $7 top-of-the-line seats in New York have me at such a distance from the court that it is almost inconceivable that a player could hear me scream. The $6 top-of-the-line seats available within a day of the game in Boston put you a linear distance of not more than fifty feet from the court, most of it in elevation. I imagine the players hear the catcalls from the balcony, some of them specifically directed. Henry Finkel of the Celtics came in for most of the abuse from the fans, but the boos turned to cheers before the game's end as the Celtics' center played well in the second half.

When the Celtics came out on the floor for the pregame warmup, the announcer shouted in excited tones, "Ladies and gentlemen, the world champion *Boston Celtics*." The Milwaukee Bucks' formation of layup lines was not acknowledged. In New York, neither team is accorded an introduction prior to the pregame announcement of the starting lineup. In Los Angeles, both teams are introduced as the Celtics are in Boston, except that the locals are always introduced as "*Your* Los Angeles Lakers!"

Any slim hope the Celtics harbored at the time they played Milwaukee of making the playoffs have since been squashed. Philadelphia has clinched the fourth and last playoff spot in the Eastern Division. For the first time in twenty years, the NBA will hold playoffs without a representative from Beantown. The adjustment to a lower status must have been difficult for the Boston fans this year, and it might be said that the interest they expressed in the game I saw is to their credit. The attendance was near 10,000, few fans left early, all seemed to be involved. Except for a woeful misunderstanding of the 3-second rule that characterized the fans most immediately surrounding me, they seemed well-informed. There was something honest about seeing a sports event without the gloss and sheen that characterizes modernized promotion. I felt, somehow, that the Boston

111

Garden had preserved the spirit of Ebbets Field and the old Madison Square Garden.

MARCH 17

The New York Knickerbockers are the champions of the NBA Eastern Division and are assured of holding that title for at least two weeks, or until the end of the first round of the playoffs. They clinched the title at San Diego on Saturday.

Considering that they are divisional winners, not too much seems to be going right for the Knicks of late. Bill Bradley's ankle has only just gotten well enough for him to play again, and the month of practice and ballgames that he missed can't do his stamina any good. Walt Frazier reinjured the groin muscle that shelved him in the playoffs last year and—while all concerned swear that it is not as serious as last year's injury—he will miss tonight's game in Detroit. Mike Riordan, Ireland's child, will get a Saint Patrick's Day start.

Since the last writing, the Knicks have won 8 and lost 5, hardly a championship pace, and they have dropped 3 out of 5 on the road. They had done particularly badly against Baltimore, Philadelphia, and Atlanta—compared with earlier performances this season—and these three teams may have to be overcome to win the playoff championship, which is the one everybody remembers. The Knicks haven't played Milwaukee and Lew Alcindor since January 2, and the Bucks are very much improved and a playoff threat. Just to make things a little more unpleasant, Wilt Chamberlain has shed his cast and will be testing his health against the Boston Celtics on Wednesday night. If the Knicks have to play the Lakers in the playoff, it will be in the last of the three best-of-seven series, and if Chamberlain is healthy enough to start playing on Wednesday, he should be a holy terror by then.

The Bradley injury has had quite a bit to do with the Knicks' problems over the past month. Cazzie Russell began filling in for Dollar Bill with a hot scoring streak, so the loss of Bradley's defensive and "boxing-out-on-the-boards" ability was somewhat mitigated. However, when Cazzie returned to the mortals as a shooter, his shortcomings became a problem. Dave Stallworth has played very well in spots, getting more court time with Bradley's injury and doing some of the things that Bradley does on defense. However, Stallworth is not Bradley, and when Stallworth is playing, obviously he can't come off the bench. The Knicks are hurting both ways.

Another way it is hurting is the increased pressure for defensive and board work that Bradley's absence places on Reed and DeBusschere. Usually, these two men have a two-on-two battle on the boards with their immediate opponents as Bradley holds one man off. Not recently. Frazier's play is affected by the loss of his favorite partner on the pick and roll and an important player in the fast-break orchestra he conducts. When a "team" is built as carefully as the Knicks and runs as smoothly, the removal of one of the parts is very keenly felt.

On the other hand, Bradley is back now. He suited up in Portland against Seattle on Friday night and played against San Diego on Saturday and Los Angeles on Sunday. The Knicks managed to win only the San Diego game, which clinched the regular-season Eastern Division crown. The emphasis now will be on getting physically and psychologically prepared for the playoffs, which begin on March 26. The season concludes with five games this week: at Detroit tomorrow, home against Milwaukee on Wednesday, at Atlanta on Friday, at home against Cincinnati on Saturday, and at Boston on Sunday afternoon. The first-

113

round opponent will be the Baltimore Bullets, with whom the Knicks split a pair of games in February. Last year the Bullets won the Eastern Division crown and the Knicks finished third. New York won the first round of the playoffs in four games. Both teams know it really will be a brand-new season.

The *Post* reports today that Willis Reed will be announced as the NBA's Most Valuable Player, as voted by the players. Jerry West, according to the same article, feels he should have been the winner of the award this year. West's reasoning, essentially, is that Reed must share credit for the Knicks' standing with Walt Frazier and Dave DeBusschere, while the many injuries the Lakers suffered required West to carry the burden alone. The Knicks reply that team standings count very much. Last year Westley Unseld of Baltimore won the MVP when many people, including almost all the Knicks, felt Reed should have won it. Last year Baltimore won the Eastern Division championship, a fact that was considered by players voting for Unseld. The Knicks feel it is only fair that the same fact was considered by players voting for Reed.

I'd hate to arbitrate this dispute. My understanding of a Most Valuable Player can best be expressed negatively—which player, if taken away from his team, would result in a distinct drop in the team's success? The Knicks would not have taken first place without Reed. It is conceivable to me that they *might* have without Frazier or DeBusschere, although it is questionable. Obviously the Lakers would have been nowhere without Jerry West. But the Milwaukee Bucks would have been just as nowhere without Lew Alcindor. In the final analysis, it is impossible to determine who the *most* valuable player is. If Chamberlain and Baylor had not been injured, would it have decreased West's value? If Frazier and Bradley had been injured more than they were, would it have increased Reed's value? Should the MVP award hinge on injuries to other players on the team of the potential winner? I think not. Jerry West is a great ballplayer and has had a great season. The Lakers unquestionably need him, and it would have been justified if he had been voted MVP. But the same can be said for Reed and the Knicks, and there can be little question that Reed, also, deserves the award. I am surprised that a man of Jerry West's caliber became involved in a dispute such as this, the only result of which is to discredit Reed, West himself, and the award.

Red Holzman is now the general manager *and* coach of the Knicks. Eddie Donovan, who built the powerhouse from the bottom up as GM, resigned to become general manager of the new expansion franchise in Buffalo. Donovan lives in Olean, New York, where he coached St. Bonaventure before coming to the Knicks, and his family has never left there. Buffalo is commuting distance from Olean, and the change is understandable. Holzman was typically noncommital in his response to the press about assuming the dual role. He doesn't know if he can handle it; he doesn't know if he cannot. He might keep both jobs for quite a while; he might do one and give up the other. My guess is that Red will keep both jobs for a season or two and then turn over the coaching to one of his current players, possibly Dave DeBusschere. The parallel developing here is to the Boston Celtics' dynasty in which Coach Red Auerbach moved to GM and installed Bill Russell as coach. The only thing that makes it unlikely that a precise parallel will result is Willis Reed's stated distaste for the job of coaching.

I dropped by the Garden yesterday to pick up tickets for the National Invitation Tournament games. LSU's Pete Maravich is in town for the college tourney and I'm anxious to see this young man who dribbles between his legs, passes off his ear, and averages about 46 points a game play his final college series. Knick playoff tickets are also on sale now and season-ticket-holders are permitted to pick up tickets for their regular seats any time this week. Not yet having gone to the bank, I was not prepared to buy my playoff tickets ($12.50/game, a $100 expenditure for two to the first round alone—you *know* basketball fans are crazy!). Instead, I was trying to puzzle out which of the twenty-odd windows in the Garden lobby would sell me Maravich tickets when a fellow walked up to me and said, "Playoff tickets are down there."

I didn't recognize him, but he obviously recognized me. Where from?

"I wonder why they won't let us get a few extra tickets for the playoffs," he said. "I'd like to get a third or fourth seat."

Still wondering who he was, I tried to answer his question. "Well, figure that about 12,000 of the 19,500 seats in the Garden are season seats. That means that if anybody could get more than than just what they purchased for the season, there wouldn't be tickets for anybody else."

"I guess you're right," he said. "Everybody in our section is season, don't you think?" I realized that he was a neighbor of mine in Section 111. I will have to look around for him at the Milwaukee game tomorrow night and find out where he sits.

MARCH 19

Despite the overwhelming sentiment expressed in the press and by the fans that last night's game against Milwaukee was critical as a harbinger of things to come in the playoffs, the Knicks played as if they didn't really care. Milwaukee saw a 20-point bulge they held for most of the game cut by a meaningless spurt in the last few minutes and won convincingly, 116–108. Lew Alcindor dominated Willis Reed, and—without Walt Frazier in the backcourt—Flynn Robinson scored almost at will. Assuming the Knicks get by Baltimore and Milwaukee can beat Philadelphia in the first round of the playoffs, Alcindor and Robinson will be two formidable obstacles in the Knicks' quest for their first NBA championship.

Bill Bradley had re-entered the lineup in meaningful form against Detroit the night before last, registering 19 points and ten assists while the Knicks ran over the hapless Pistons. Bradley played more than 30 minutes last night at forward and guard, more minutes than any other Knick regular registered, but was not tremendously impressive. His shooting and timing seem to have suffered from the long layoff caused by his ankle injury. With Frazier out and Dave DeBusschere playing only briefly in the first quarter, the Knicks were no match for the Bucks. The papers today report that DeBusschere was "weak," but the weakness was not attributed to a specific cause. We fans must assume, on the basis of terribly inadequate reportage, that there is nothing to worry about.

Last night, for what took place on the floor and in the stands, was just not the most pleasurable for me. I have been putting up with a lot of kidding and stupid questions from a bunch of fans behind me who are aware that this book is being written. These gentlemen occupy four seats, although there are more than four of them (they share the tickets). In any case, they seem determined to convince everybody within earshot that they are wild, fanatic, knowledgeable Knickerbocker fans of the top order.

The kidding began a couple of weeks ago when Bradley was injured and I was besieged, several times a game, with questions about his injury. I knew little more than what we all read in the papers. For all the troubles I have had with them, Blauschild and Wergeles do maintain close touch with Holzman and Whelan and try to feed up-to-date and accurate information to the press on injuries. Bradley's ankle

117

was a day-to-day proposition for a couple of weeks. The press reported it that way, and doubtless Holzman, Whelan and Bradley felt that way. It is understandable that many Knick fans felt there was more to be known, especially with the playoffs coming up and the report on Bradley's health not changing as his absence continued. I accepted the first inquiry from these fans and politely begged off by saying I knew no more than they.

Still, the questioning persisted, moving on to somewhat tasteless insults. Dan, by this time, had also had his fill of the annoying commentary from behind and started tossing dry sarcasm over his shoulder, most of which was obviously going over their heads. Then, about a week ago, one of the men brought a loud, raucous, obnoxious, childish air horn to a game. I turned around and said, "That's cheap-seat stuff. People who pay good money to sit close to a basketball game don't play with kid toys like that." That only provoked the gentlemen further, so I gave up protesting, hoping they would just get tired of the horn.

I was no sooner seated last night when one of the fellows leaned over and said, "I'm sorry I forgot that horn tonight."

"I'm not sorry," I said, not turning to face him and wishing he'd disappear.

The game went on below us, with the Knicks falling further behind as the seconds ticked off the clock. Frazier was hurt and, due to the preparation for the playoffs, Riordan and Barnett were getting a lot of rest. Bradley, who needs more playing time to get back into shape, was playing guard. At halftime, one of my friends leaned forward to start the conversation again.

"What do you think is the significance of Bradley playing guard?"

I swear that's how he phrased it. I couldn't decide whether it sounded more like a question from a college exam or the inquiry of one of the eight-year-old kids who call up the radio talk shows to suggest baseball-player trades that would send young general managers to early graves. "I'd say the significance is that Frazier is hurt, Barnett and Riordan are tired, and the rules still say you need five men."

"Yeah, but don't you think that the Knicks might be planning to use him at guard so they can leave Riordan unprotected in the expansion draft."

"I don't think so," I said, trying hard to phrase it so that nobody would think I had information I didn't have. "I think you can use Bradley as a guard during an emergency, but I don't think you can consider him a guard in the overall picture or in your planning." I was satisfied with the answer, but these guys weren't. They tore apart my point of view in a stage whisper designed for my hearing but not for my response for the rest of the game.

Even Max—friendly Max, who has been a great neighbor all season—got into the act last night. Max has this anti-Mike Riordan thing that he's been pushing since the beginning of the season. I think it all comes from Max's unswerving faith in "good shooting." It is Max's contention that you can't be taken seriously as a pro-basketball player if you don't hit an open shot inside 20 feet at least ten times out of nine. Of course, if pros all made Max's standard, each team would average 180 points a game. Riordan is not a top-notch outside shooter for a guard, but he has improved his outside shooting and the rest of his play so much this year that he can be legitimately considered the second-best sub guard in the league (to Philadelphia's Wally Jones). Max doesn't think so.

Well, Max knows I don't agree with him, and I can't help thinking he's worried that I'll make Riordan look too good in my book if he doesn't educate me in a hurry. Last night he pointed out every error, real and imagined, that Riordan made and punctuated his information with "and *that's* why he'll never make it as a pro guard." The king of all these insane comments came while the Knicks were pressing the Bucks in the fourth quarter, trying to whittle a big deficit down to respectability for the box score.

Milwaukee was spreading their guards very wide in the forecourt, about thirty feet apart and each near a sideline. As soon as the ball crossed midcourt, the Knicks would double-team the guard with the ball, trying to force the play to remain on one side. If this press works, it effectively cuts the forecourt in half, making steals much easier and penetration by the offense much more difficult. The problem with the press—as with any other double-team—is that *somebody* is left open. The advantage to *this* press, as opposed to other presses, is that the man who is left open is a guard who is some twenty-five feet from the basket. Riordan, adhering to the strategy, left the man he was guarding to double-team. The man he was guarding was Jon McGlocklin, one of Milwaukee's best outside shooters. Max was up in arms. *"Don't* leave McGlocklin open, you dummy," he shouted. He turned to me. "He can't think quick out there. And *that's* why he'll never make it as a pro guard." Max triumphantly rested his case while I just shook my head.

The potential playoff problems grow daily. Wilt Chamberlain played for the Lakers against the Celtics last night and the wire-service reports in the *Post* indicate that he may well be in top shape before the Knicks might see the Lakers again, in the last round of the playoffs, two or three weeks from now. If Chamberlain is *not* in top shape, the Atlanta Hawks will probably win the playoffs in the West, and they have given the Knicks trouble this year, with the most difficulties coming in the most recent games. The Knicks have another "harbinger" game against the Hawks in Atlanta on Friday night, and Frazier will not make the trip.

In the East, the Knicks have other worries. They must beat Baltimore, over whom they stand 5–1 for the season.

The one loss the Knicks suffered at the Bullets' hands was also recent, however, and the domination over Baltimore that was exercised since before the first round of the 1969 playoff may have been exorcised by the Bullets prior to this year's first round. After Baltimore, the Knicks must face either Philadelphia, one of the toughest teams for them, or Milwaukee. Since the 23–1 start, the Knicks stand 37–18 and Milwaukee 42–15. It's a good thing the season started in October, not December.

MARCH 24

I think the Knicks managed to scare the hell out of everybody before they finished their regular season. They lost their last four—to Milwaukee, Atlanta, Cincinnati, and Boston—playing at various times without Walt Frazier and Willis Reed.

Frazier missed both the Milwaukee and Atlanta losses, both of which were decisive without the Knicks' ball-mover in the lineup. The cause of Walt's absence was a recurrence of the groin injury that sidelined him during the postseason playoffs last season, which ultimately saw the Knicks lose in the second round to Boston.

Reed missed the season's finale at Boston on Sunday with an aching knee. Red Holzman expressed little concern during a halftime interview from Boston about Reed's soreness. Maybe everybody else's fears were allayed, but mine were not. Edgar Lacey of UCLA played on a hurting knee for a while during the 1965–66 season, and when they X-rayed it they found a hairline fracture that finished him for the season. Reed's X-ray turned out negative, however, and it looks like he'll be ready for the opener of the playoff against Baltimore on Thursday.

As if there weren't enough things to worry about, today's

Post reports that Cazzie Russell may not be available for all of the playoff games. The strike of postal employees led President Nixon to call up some reserve units to move the mail, and Cazzie's unit was among those pressed into service. It is not yet definite that Cazzie will miss any game, but he'll have responsibilities that might conflict.

The world championship that seemed inevitable during October and November now seems distant, though not unlikely. Atlanta took the season series from the Knicks, winning the last four of the six games between the teams. And Milwaukee beat New York the last two times the teams met. In addition, a four-game losing streak hardly indicates the proper momentum going into the most important stretch of the season.

The parallel between this season and last is uncanny as far as Baltimore and New York are concerned, only the roles are reversed. The 1968–69 Bullets enjoyed a pennant-winning season, slumping toward the end as their star forward, Gus Johnson, was sidelined with an injury. Baltimore led by MVP center Wes Unseld, had to face the then third-place Knicks in the first round of the playoffs.

The 1969–70 Knicks tore the league apart early on their way to the Eastern Division crown, but an injury to star forward Bill Bradley interrupted their momentum. They now face third-place Baltimore, and the Knicks will rely on their MVP center, Willis Reed.

Reed's MVP award is the only individual honor that New York seems likely to capture this year. The final statistics for the season, just released, show few Knicks among the individual leaders. Jerry West was the league's top scorer at 31.1 points per game. No Knick finished in the top ten. Johnny Green of Cincinnati had the best field-goal percentage, .559, and no Knick is listed in the top five. Flynn Robinson was the most accurate foul-shooter, hitting .898, and no Knick placed in the top five. Elvin Hayes of San Diego

122

averaged 16.9 rebounds a game, and no Knick was in the top five. Walt Frazier finished second to Len Wilkins of Seattle in assists, averaging 8.2 to Wilkins' 9.1. The absence of Knick names from the lists of individual leadership only underlines the "teamwork" involved in the season's success.

Meanwhile, the league as a whole is having trouble. The ABA signed several of the top graduating collegians before the NBA draft—conducted yesterday—had even taken place. Charlie Scott of North Carolina, Dan Issel of Kentucky, and Mike Maloy of Davidson were all signed by the ABA over a week ago, and rumors indicate that the younger league has the inside track on Pete Maravich. Among the handful of acknowledge top players, only Bob Lanier of St. Bonaventure seems headed for the NBA.

The Knicks, choosing seventeenth in each round because they had the best record in the league, did not get the right to anybody terribly exciting or well-known. Mike Price of Illinois was the Knicks' first pick and a great number of the selections were local talent: John Marren of Manhattan, Jim Oxley of Army, Jim Signorile of NYU, and Ray Hodge of Wagner. Even with the thinning of the club that will occur with the expansion draft, chances that any of the newcomers will become a bulwark of the 1970–71 team are slim.

To add to the league's difficulties, the new owners of the expansion franchise in Houston failed to come up with the necessary dollars and were dropped. That means that the league will operate next year with seventeen teams and, according to current plans, four divisions. Splitting into four divisions is a strategy borrowed from football and baseball and is based on the theory that a last-place team that is fourth will do better at the box office than a last-place team that is eighth.

There has been considerable griping among the fans who sit around me about the price of the playoff tickets, scaled down from $12.50. And the way the Garden structured their availability was another target of discontent. All season-ticket-holders received an IBM card with their ticket location printed on it. In order to preserve the right to buy tickets for any round of the playoffs, the season-ticket-holder must buy them for every round. When I bought my tickets for the first round, a punch was made on my IBM card. Without that punch on my card, I would not be able to buy my ticket for the second round, if the Knicks get that far.

In the Eastern Division, the forced purchase is not so outrageous. Despite the price, which is a bit high, I will see games against Baltimore in the first round, and Baltimore is a good team. Pity Laker and Hawk season-ticker-holders, however, if they are subjected to the same conditions. Los Angeles meets Phoenix and Atlanta faces Chicago, and there is no way in the world that Phoenix or Chicago is worth inflated prices. However, the Laker fan, under the same conditions, who passed up the Phoenix series might miss an opportunity to see Atlanta or New York.

MARCH 30

Just when it was beginning to look as if the Knicks might beat Baltimore in four games again this year, the New Yorkers fell on their faces in the third game of the series yesterday. Not only did the Bullets win a one-sided 127–113 victory to cut the series margin to 2–1, New York, but Westley Unseld took down four more rebounds than the entire New York team. That is never supposed to happen, and nobody seems to remember when it ever did.

The first game of the playoff, last Thursday night, was a classic ballgame in a classic setting. The Garden was packed to the rafters, of course, and the fans were keyed to an emotional frenzy before the game began. The noise exceeded that of the regular season when the Knicks rebounded from an early 12–2 deficit to lead 14–13 halfway through the first period. The game continued very close, with the Knicks in precarious command throughout the second half. But Baltimore caught New York and passed them before the final buzzer—until Bill Bradley hit a baseline drive to knot the game at 102 and send it into overtime.

In the overtime period, Baltimore took the lead again, paced by the shooting of Earl Monroe, who finished with 39 points. Walt Frazier guarded Monroe through most of the contest and, clearly, the Bullets' star had the best of the matchup. However, Walt recouped his ball-stealing ability in the "knick" of time to send the game into a second overtime period. Fouled on the shot after one Frazier steal, Dick Barnet hit two free throws to tie the game at 110. A second Frazier steal, both from Monroe, sprung Barnett for a layup try at the buzzer, but the shot rolled off the rim to leave the contest tied and headed for a second overtime.

By this time the fans were absolutely frantic. Baltimore had played better in the playoff opener than they had in any game against the Knicks all season. The Knicks were playing their game—running, double-teaming on defense, shooting well and penetrating—but had no more than a tie at the end of a full game plus 5 minutes. A basketball purist with no particular interest in who won could contentedly have called for a stop to the contest, declaring it a magnificent exhibition that rightfully should end in a tie. A basketball fan, however, cannot be a purist. The 19,500 people in the Garden were looking for a Knick victory.

In the second overtime, Willis Reed gave it to them. The Knicks took an early lead and widened the gap to as much as 5 points before the Bullets rallied to tie the game again at 117. Then Willis Reed took off from the foul line ahead of Gus Johnson, the Bullet who was guarding him. Johnson had run a substantial risk by attempting to steal the pass to

Willis, and the Knick captain made the failure hurt. He drove down the lane and dropped the ball neatly through, giving the Knicks the points they needed for victory. The Bullets had time for one more Monroe-versus-Frazier confrontation in an attempt to tie the score again, but the Knick guard was now equal to the task. He forced Monroe to take a bad shot and New York recovered possession. Dave DeBusschere hit a foul shot to make the final score, 120–117.

DeBusschere was the big star for New York in the first game. He seemed to be involved in contesting every rebound; he defensed Baltimore's star forward, Gus Johnson, to distraction; he made key passes and key shots. Had the game ended before the 10 extra minutes, DeBusschere's heroics would have been unrivaled by the play of his teammates. As it was, the defense by Frazier and the basket by Reed were indispensable parts of the victory, but DeBusschere's accomplishments cannot be minimized. He scored 20 points and captured 24 rebounds, demonstrating over and over again his importance to the Knicks' winning machinery.

The second game of the series was played in Baltimore on Friday night and televised back to New York. In another superbly played game, the Knicks won, 106–99. Baltimore opened an early lead and maintained a modest advantage throughout the first half. A spurt paced by Monroe in the third quarter widened New York's disadvantage to 9 points at one stage, and the Knicks trailed by 6, 83–77, at the end of that period.

But then Mike Riordan, Knick hero for the day, stepped to the fore and hit two quick buckets to start the Knicks' fourth-quarter drive. Riordan did it all, filling in for a tiring Dick Barnett, as he scored 13 points while shutting off Earl Monroe. Mixed in with his other heroics were eight very important rebounds, all key elements in the final New York success.

It was fiitting that DeBusschere and Riordan made the key contributions to the two New York victories in the play-offs, since their play has not been as well-appreciated by the fans during the season as that of more flashy teammates. Both DeBusschere and Riordan excel on defense, a phase of the game that is far more reliable than offense. They don't slump in their specialty. They give a good perform-ance game after game. However, both are erratic shooters and have had their share of games where they hit a very low percentage of their shots. DeBusschere is a starter and always guards the top opposing forward, so he does get some of the attention he deserves from the fans—although not as much as he should. Riordan, however, comes into the game for Dick Barnett or Walt Frazier, two of the flashiest offensive ballplayers you'd ever want to see, and Mike has a tougher road to hoe to get the attention he deserves. A good showing in the playoffs is usually remembered, how-ever, and Mike might hear considerably more cheers next year if he continues to play as he did in Baltimore.

If the first two games of the series were well-played, close contests, the third was a disaster for the Knicks. The Bullets opened up an early lead before Walt Frazier, on his twenty-fifth birthday, got hot to move the Knicks in front with a flurry of baskets at the end of the first quarter and the beginning of the second. But the lead was short-lived. The 64–63 lead the Knicks held at halftime vanished during a third-quarter blitz by the Bullets, during which the Knicks couldn't hit a shot and the Bullets were throwing them in from every conceivable angle. Unseld's rebounding was the headline, but certainly not the whole story. Earl Monroe scored 25 points for Baltimore, which got 23 from Unseld and Fred Carter and 20 from Jack Marin.

The Knicks did not shoot for a bad percentage, 46-for-95 from the floor, but they seldom got a second shot on any offensive sortie. Willis Reed played only 29 minutes due to recurring foul trouble, DeBusschere appeared tired, and

Unseld had the boards pretty much to himself. The series goes back to Baltimore tomorrow night, and the fifth game will be at the Garden on Thursday night. Unless the Knicks win both games, the series will continue in Baltimore on Sunday and maybe New York on Monday.

In the other playoff quarter-finals going on, both the Milwaukee–Philadelphia series and the Los Angeles–Phoenix series are 1–1. Atlanta took the first two from Chicago. The Lakers may be in trouble: Chamberlain had a very bad game in the loss to Phoenix, whose Connie Hawkins can turn a seven-game series around by himself. Lew Alcindor won the first game for Milwaukee against the 76ers, and Billy Cunningham returned the favor against the Bucks, scoring 37 points. These two players are the keys to their teams' chances.

The Knicks had their six-game playoff winning streak against Baltimore snapped by yesterday's loss, but there is no critical danger yet. Everybody on the ballclub is healthy, with the possible exception of Bill Hosket, who turned an ankle slightly pinch-hitting for Reed yesterday. For five halves out of six in the three games, the team defense and quick offense have been in top condition, too, and Baltimore will have to win another ballgame before I'll believe their chances in this series are for real. The Bullets played two superlative games in their losses to New York and Westley Unseld paced an unbelievable one in the Bullet victory. Even at a pace that must be a peak for even the Bullets' exceptional ability, they trail in the series, 2–1. There are no indications of an imminent Knickerbocker collapse.

APRIL 6

The Knickerbockers faced their first truly critical game of the season last Thursday and all of them, led by Willis Reed, responded admirably to the pressure. The Bullets were defeated 101–80 as the Knicks took a 3–2 edge in the playoff series.

Baltimore's cold shooting and the dominating play of Reed were the most important factors contributing to the Knick rout. Willis scored 36 points and captured 36 rebounds as he outmuscled Wes Unseld time and time again for position under the basket. Dave DeBusschere continued to do top-notch defensive work on Gus Johnson, holding him to 7 points. DeBusschere kept Johnson off the offensive boards by shooting from the outside. Dave was not hitting in Thursday's game, but he is a good enough outside shooter that Johnson felt obliged to guard him even out to the 20-foot range. DeBusschere is probably a step quicker than Johnson, and he won the race to the offensive boards from that distance. Strong as Dave is, he probably does not match Gus Johnson for strength, and the Knick forward must keep moving to use his speed advantage to make it to the boards.

Baltimore's shooting fell apart completely in the fourth quarter, during which they hit only three field goals and scored 11 points in 12 minutes. The Knicks' defense played well throughout the game but could never have held Baltimore to 80 points without some help from a cold Bullet offense.

As the series resumed in Baltimore yesterday afternoon, it looked for all the world like the Bullets had not regained their shooting eyes. Unfortunately, the Knicks were also shooting badly in the early going and could not open up a substantial lead. The Knicks led, 18–15, at the end of the first quarter and by only 2 points, 43–41, at the end of the first half. Actually, the Knicks were fortunate to be ahead at all. Dave DeBusschere picked up three very fast personal fouls and Dave Stallworth had to come in to handle Gus Johnson. Stallworth is quick and talented, but Johnson's mammoth strength almost requires a bull like DeBusschere to guard him. Stallworth did all right, however, and pumped in a couple of shots of his own, so the Knicks did not lose by the temporary exchange.

In the second half, however, Johnson and Earl Monroe recovered their eyes for the hoop and the Bullets were not to be denied. Gus pumped in three baskets immediately after intermission and Baltimore was off and running. The Knick deficit stretched to as much as 10 points, 62–52, before they whittled it down to 71–66 at the end of the third quarter.

Walt Frazier, whose offensive work has been limited during the past couple of games but who has played great defense on Earl Monroe, hit a jumper to open the fourth quarter and the Knicks trailed by only 3 points. But then they fell behind again by a wide margin before fighting back to within 6, 89–83, with a couple of minutes to go. Then Bill Bradley stole a pass and went downcourt on a 2-on-1 break with Mike Riordan. Bradley passed to Riordan, who missed the shot, and then Bradley missed the rebound. The failure to capitalize on this particular opportunity cut off the momentum for a Knick comeback, and Baltimore won, 96–87, to square the series.

As for tonight's game, the sportswriters and sportscasters would say, "There is no tomorrow." The Knicks are faced with a "must-win" situation, if they are to capture their first world championship. There is something very cruel about a system that puts the whole thing on the line in one game, regardless of past performances, heroics, accomplishments. But such is the case. The Bullets, who must have been terribly discouraged after losing the first two games in this series, now find that they need only one more win for a fresh start. According to Holzman and the Knick players, the home-town fans have been a great help throughout the season. There will be 19,500 screaming their heads off at the Garden tonight. On the other hand, the Bullets were not expected to win this series, so they might be just a bit looser than the Knicks.

Milwaukee finished its series with Philadelphia in five games, winning the last three. Lew Alcindor, as expected, carried the load—and regardless of whether the Knicks or Bullets win tonight, the winner will face a zealous, well-rested Buck team later in the week.

Atlanta knocked off Chicago in five games and now awaits the winner of the Phoenix–Los Angeles series. That one is beginning to look like the bloody mess the Knick–Bullet series has turned into, with the Suns leading the favored Lakers 3–2 after Los Angeles came on for a "must" win last night. The Hawks, strong, deep, and with the home-court advantage they will have for finishing first, will have the added advantage of more rest over either the Suns or the Lakers. The Hawks will be almost impossible to stop in their division.

J. WALTER KENNEDY

The National Basketball Association occupies a small suite of offices at 2 Pennsylvania Plaza five floors above a much larger suite occupied by the Madison Square Garden Corporation. I arrived early for my appointment with Commissioner Kennedy and overheard a secretary ask a graying but athletic-looking man in a business suit who the two best referees in the NBA were. He replied, "Rudolph and Powers." I found out later that he was Richie Powers and, as it turned out, he and Mendy Rudolph worked that evening's Knick-Bullet game.

If the suite of offices the NBA occupies is small, the office occupied by the Commissioner himself is not. Across from the Commissioner, I sat looking out a window with a stunning view of Manhattan. Mr. Kennedy apologized for the telephone interruptions he anticipated, which did indeed occur. One of the callers wanted tickets for that night's playoff game. (The Commissioner spent some time studying the few tickets he had and finally fulfilled the request, although he couldn't give his caller four tickets together.) One caller I surmised was Marty Blake, the general manager of the Atlanta Hawks, and he and the Commissioner discussed the network-television schedule. The Hawks' playoff game next weekend has been set to be nationally aired, and Kennedy cleared some questions up for Blake on that score.

Between the calls, the Commissioner talked about the structure of the league. "The NBA is a joint venture, a nonprofit organization of the NBA teams. We have a long constitution and by-laws by which we operate, the league 'bible.' My job is to administer that bible."

The Denny McLain incident and related gambling investigations have aroused considerable public interest in professional sports' security operations. Kennedy seemed eager to outline the NBA procedure. "We have an outside investigative staff, have had them for several years. If they turn up anything that requires my attention, they let me know. Then I settle it with the player involved or possibly the player's team."

I wondered if Kennedy had any second thoughts about the restrictions placed on professional athletes that might infringe on their civil liberties. Kennedy was quite strong on this point.

"Each season since I have been Commissioner, since 1963, I have gone to every training camp before the season and talked briefly to all the players. I advise them that after they signed an NBA contract, they lost their status as a private citizen and they became *special* citizens. As NBA players, or special citizens, they have special responsibilities. They cannot, for example, associate with known gamblers or frequent questionable places. After the first week of the season, I send a personal letter to every player—this is after the last cut—quoting the constitution and his contract, citing all the obligations he has as to his conduct.

"To give you an example of what I mean, a player who is approached and asked to unduly affect the outcome of a game and who does not report this *immediately* to his coach is subject to a lifetime suspension. I do have the power to suspend him from basketball for the rest of his life."

What about officials? Do they have similar obligations?

"Even more so," Kennedy said. He mused for a second and smiled. "Well, it can't really be *more* so, but obviously the referees are under similar strict regulations of conduct."

Kennedy talked about the skepticism of some fans that the games are always on the up-and-up. "This comes of ignorance and frustration," he said. "I'll give you two examples.

"I was waiting for the train in Stamford, where I live, and I overheard two men on the platform talking. They didn't know who I was. They were talking about the Knicks' series having gone seven games and commenting that the players might have allowed this deliberately to make more money from more games. Well, you know as well as I do that the players' pool is established before the playoffs even begin and they don't make any extra money whether they win in four games or seven.

"Then in the elevator two men from this floor were saying that for some reason the league was trying to create an Atlanta–Milwaukee final. Comments like that just don't make any sense!"

I tried to find out what Kennedy's thoughts were on the oft-discussed and currently active merger negotiations with the ABA. He waved the question with his hand. "This is for a book, isn't it? Look, by the time this book comes out, the question will be settled. I don't expect a merger, but the problem will be resolved, one way or the other, in the next couple of months."

Kennedy ran a public-relations firm starting in 1946, and the NBA was a client of his from its inception in 1946 until 1951. "It just got too big to be handled as an account." He maintained his interest in sports throughout the Fifties and it outlasted his public-relations business. In 1959 he was elected Mayor of Stamford, Connecticut.

"It was in 1962 that I was first approached about becoming Commissioner. I had just been re-elected in Stamford, and I couldn't really consider it. Finally, though, the offer was made so attractive that I couldn't turn it down. I started on September 1, 1963, with a three-year contract. After two years the owners tore it up and gave me a five-year contract. Then in June of 1968 I got a new five-year contract. Last January they voted another new five-year contract, which will take affect in June of this year."

Kennedy talked about his original goals when he became the Commissioner. "There were two things that I considered paramount when I took office. First of all, the league needed wider television coverage. At that time there was no national television contract. We got one very quickly after I took office.

"The second goal was an orderly expansion from the nine teams we had then to twenty teams. We are still working under that expansion program and next year we will have seventeen teams. I think the expansion has done very well. Look, it is still possible that our two youngest teams, Milwaukee and Phoenix, will meet in the championship finals, and those two clubs are among the best draws in the league, along with Seattle, another recent addition. We thought it would take five years for the Chicago franchise to turn the corner—they have done it in four years.

"We advise new owners to meet with existing owners to get promotional ideas that will work in their areas. Milwaukee, for example, has several thousand season-ticket-holders and Phoenix is lucky if it has 1,500. Both franchises are doing well, but they work differently. Most of the men who become new franchise-holders are either well-versed in sports promotion before they begin or very quickly hire somebody who is."

The Commissioner has a very definite program for over-seeing his domain. "I guess I see about a hundred games a year, including the playoffs. I try to get to the West Coast at the beginning of the season and get to the Midwest shortly afterward so I have been in all the league cities by the first of the year. Then I visit them all again before the season ends. When I make these swings I talk to club officials and general managers and find out if there is anything in the way of information and communication that they need from the league office that they're not getting. We point out magazine articles they might be interested in, for example. And we receive about forty newspapers a day here in the office. Nick Curran, the league public-relations man, photocopies any articles of interest that a club might miss and gets it to them."

Generally, the teams in the NBA enjoy a great deal of autonomy from the league office. "The teams set their own ticket prices, even for the playoffs, although we urge them to set higher prices than they had during the regular season. In the first year, there was some reluctance to increase prices for the playoffs, but since it has worked well for everybody, the consultation between the teams and the league on ticket prices is very brief. The league picks up all the expenses for the playoffs: hotel, meals, and travel for all the players, coaches, and officials, and we pay the play-off pools. To cover these expenses, we take a set percentage from the playoff receipts. This varies from year to year and we work it out based on our projections before the playoffs of costs and revenue. Otherwise, we take a straight 6 percent assessment of the gate after taxes during the season to run the league office."

Despite the phone calls and interruptions by NBA staffers who had problems for the Commissioner, he was most polite during our conversation, never indicating that he didn't have all the time in the world to talk about his job. He didn't surprise me a bit with his answer when I asked him how he liked it.

"I love it. It's not a job for somebody who likes short hours or who ducks decision-making. But I've always worked long hours—been a six-hour-a-night man for twenty-five years. I was the full-time Mayor of a city of 110,000 people with all the one-man problems that involves. It was a great training ground, not that I needed it. There is no amount of money that could make this job attractive to somebody who didn't love it, although my owners are very generous with me. You have to enjoy the work, and I do."

As I left, the Commissioner emphasized that he would be happy to speak with me again if I needed any more information. The offer was exceedingly generous, considering the vivid picture that he had already given. The Commissioner of the NBA is a lucky man—he has a singular, unique job. There is only one American president and one United Nations secretary-general. And there is only one NBA commissioner—a splendid and glamorous fact that is not lost on J. Walter Kennedy. But like his brothers who are at the top of different pyramids, the responsibilities and workload are awesome. His job offers an almost unchecked power for which he must pay with an equally unbridled devotion.

APRIL 8

It may have occurred to players on the Knicks, as it occurred to me shortly before the seventh game of the series with the

Bullets, that the whole season came down to this one game. The frustrating part of that realization was that, even with the game being won, this would be true for more games in later series. Walt Frazier was quoted as wishing that the championship could be decided by one game. It was the night-after-night pressure that got to him.

The pressure certainly did not interfere with Frazier's play. His defensive work on Earl Monroe, coupled with the offensive explosions of Dave DeBusschere, Dick Barnett, and Cazzie Russell, spearheaded the Knicks' 127–113 victory. DeBusschere, Barnett, and Russell had all been offensively dormant throughout the Baltimore series. Their sudden, welcome eruption allowed the Knicks to achieve their decisive victory without much scoring from Willis Reed and Bill Bradley.

The crowd was keyed to a fever pitch before the game began, and the signs that their enthusiasm was having its effects on the Knicks' play were evident from the start. The slender 28–23 lead the Knicks' held at the end of the first quarter was due only to Baltimore's good play. The Bullets seemed to have the attitude that since few people had expected them to get this close to beating the Knicks, it seemed a shame to get so far and lose.

But the brilliant team defense and sharp shooting by DeBusschere and Barnett were not to be denied. A series of steals and fast breaks in the second quarter, continuing as all the regulars were substituted for, allowed the Knicks to open up a 60–45 lead by halftime. The most beautiful play during this spurt was executed by DeBusschere and Bradley. Dave intercepted a cross-court pass by Baltimore and drove straight down the court and bounced a perfect pass to Bradley, coming down on the left side. Bradley caught the pass ahead of Fred Carter, the Baltimore defender, and scored on a difficult layup, going in at top speed and with no time between receiving the pass and reaching the basket for any ball-juggling or weight-shifting. That play, combined with several defensive efforts by Walt Frazier, opened up the 15-point advantage.

Through most of the third quarter, the Knicks held on to their big lead, matching the hot Bullets almost shot for shot. DeBusschere and Reed were doing very well on the boards whenever Baltimore missed. The Knicks let up a bit at quarter's end and it almost cost them dearly. Baltimore closed the gap to 88–82 before heading into the final 12 minutes. Ordinarily, a 6-point lead against as good an offensive team as Baltimore would be little with 12 minutes to go, but the fans around me registered fairly little concern. The Knicks have yet to lose a game this season when they have played well—they are too good a team for that. And the fourth quarter had barely started when the lead was opened up again. Baltimore tried to press throughout the last 5 minutes, but the Knicks handled it easily.

The prevailing sentiment—except on the part of the Baltimore players—is that Milwaukee will be tougher. One of the Bullets was quoted as saying that the Knicks should go all the way now, since the Bullets and the Knicks are the two best teams in the NBA. This is probably true. Despite the fact that Milwaukee was terribly impressive in swamping Philadelphia, 4 games to 1, it seems unlikely that the Bucks will be as much trouble as the Bullets. Milwaukee relies primarily on two men for their offensive punch, Lew Alcindor and Flynn Robinson. The Knicks' "team defense" thrives when offensive weaknesses allow them to double- or triple-team certain players without leaving good shooters open. Baltimore frequently foiled this strategy because of the number of good shooters they have. All the Baltimore starters shoot well from outside, and their top offensive gun, Earl Monroe, is more potent and elusive than the Bucks' Robinson. In addition, the Bullets' defensive matchups allow them to play the Knicks well, particuarly with Unseld's strength against Reed's and Gus Johnson's muscle against DeBusschere's.

The key to the series will be the success of Lew Alcindor on Willis. Alcindor had a fabulous series against Philadelphia, taking Darrall Imhoff apart in sections almost at will. While nobody can stop Lew when he is "on" and tossing in hook shots, he may have trouble playing well consistently against Reed. Willis is stronger and more experienced than Alcindor, and in a short, intense series those two advantages may more than make up for Lew's height advantages. On top of that, neither Bob Dandridge nor Greg Smith, the Milwaukee forwards, shoot well enough from outside to keep DeBusschere and Bradley from harassing Alcindor. In only one of the four victories against Baltimore did Willis Reed figure as an offensive bulwark. If he can neutralize Alcindor, the remaining firepower that the Knicks offer should end the Milwaukee series more quickly than the seven games it took to elminate Baltimore.

An important item in the last Bullet victory was the excellent play of Cazzie Russell. There have been many other instances this year of Cazzie coming off the bench to score quickly and furiously. What made his performance in the last Baltimore game thrilling and encouraging was his good defensive and rebounding play. The Knicks can go to Cazzie even more against Milwaukee, if the need for points should become acute, because his defensive weaknesses are compensated by the offensive weakness of Milwaukee's forwards. Even Len Chappell, a Milwaukee forward who can shoot and who had one brilliant game in their series with Philadelphia, should not be impossible for Cazzie to guard. Russell's problem is one of lateral movement—speed —and Chappell is very slow, albeit a good shooter.

The Knicks have earned the home-court advantage for every series in the playoffs by having the best regular-season record in the NBA. The encouragement that the crowd has

139

offered seems to have been extremely helpful thus far and —all other things being equal—could provide the margin of victory in any series en route to the championship. Against Atlanta, should the Hawks win the West, this could be critical. Against Milwaukee there is a lot more than the crowd going for the Knicks.

APRIL 14

I stopped into a coffee shop near the Garden last night before the second game of the Knick–Buck series and found myself seated at a table with a man and his son who were talking basketball. The kid was about fourteen years old and had clearly been following the Knicks for quite some time, considering his age. I asked him who his favorite player was. "Walt Frazier." Absolutely no hesitation. Did all his friends like Frazier best? "No, I think a lot like Willis Reed, but I figure I'll never grow that tall and if I want to be a pro ballplayer I'll have to be like Walt Frazier."

Regardless of favorite players, the favorite team of just about everybody in the Garden last night achieved its second victory over the Bucks, 112–111, and departs for the next pair of games in Milwaukee with a 2–0 lead. Both Frazier and Reed were dazzling last night, in completely different departments. Reed carried the Knicks' scoring load throughout the game, picking up 21 points in the first half on his way to a game total of 36 and helping out further with nineteen rebounds. For the second-straight game Frazier did not score well—he notched 10 last night and 6 in the series opener on Saturday—but he excelled at everything else. Walt got twelve rebounds, more than DeBusschere, Bradley, and Stallworth combined, and handed off fourteen assists. The two together led a "just-enough"

Knicks' performance. Lew Alcindor scored 38 points and took 23 rebounds, passing off 11 assists, and brought the Bucks to within 1 point of victory. However, two foul shots that Lew missed in the final minute assured the Milwaukee defeat.

The opening game of the series was almost all Knicks. They won 110–102, but the final score was only close because of a Bucks' rally in the fourth quarter that never seriously threatened to overtake the Knicks. Reed played well against Lew in the opener, but the Bucks' star clearly had the statistical edge. The other Bucks just didn't contribute. Walt Frazier harassed Flynn Robinson into a 4-for-16 shooting performance and Milwaukee's other standout guard, Jon McGlocklin, only managed to get off nine shots against Dick Barnett and Mike Riordan. The bench did well, with the Knicks increasing their advantage during Nate Bowman's appearance in the second quarter. Bowman handles Alcindor well defensively, better than he handles any other center in the league. It is difficult to explain a phenomenon of this sort, but there are several possible reasons for it. First of all, Bowman has good height and long arms. This allows him to harass Alcindor when Lew holds the ball high, such as when he hooks. Secondly, Reed plays Alcindor totally differently than Bowman does—using muscle whereas Bowman uses height—and the difference may be difficult for Alcindor to accommodate to in the brief time that Bowman plays and Reed rests.

What really helped the Knicks open up a big lead on the Bucks in the first game was their ability to sag to the middle, double-teaming Alcindor when he had the ball and fronting him effectively when he did not, thus making it very difficult for the Bucks to work it in to him. The best antidote for this type of defense is for Lew to pass quickly off the pivot to the man who should be guarded by the

Knick who is double-teaming him. The Knicks try to complicate the problem by switching assignments when they double-team, putting the open man in the most difficult position for a pass. What the Bucks' open man has to do is cut to the basket. In Saturday's game, the Bucks simply did not do what they had to do.

Last night they did. Greg Smith, an atrocious shooter but fantastic leaper who plays the rebounding forward for Milwaukee at 6-foot-4, hit six field goals, most of them after quick passes from the double-teamed Alcindor found Smith alone and waiting in the close vicinity of the basket. As the Knicks became conscious of Smith and the possibility that the alert Alcindor might hit even better shooters—McGlocklin, Dandridge, and Chappell—it made Alcindor more effective. In the third quarter, Willis Reed picked up four personal fouls within the last six minutes trying to handle Alcindor inside. Fortunately for the Knicks, Willis had not picked up any personals in the first half and did not pick up his fifth foul until near game's end, so he played until the final buzzer.

Cazzie Russell continues to play well, superbly on offense and adequately on defense. Caz pumped 18 points through the hoop in the opener, the same number that Bradley and DeBusschere each managed in considerably more playing time. What's more, Cazzie's defensive shortcomings are not as blatant against the Milwaukee forwards as they were against Jack Marin of Baltimore (just as I predicted they would not be). In the second game, Cazzie scored 12 points in 20 minutes, including the two foul shots near the half-minute mark of the fourth quarter that sealed the victory. Russell did have his bad moment, blowing a totally uncontested layup on a fast break started by a steal by Dave DeBusschere. It appeared—and Cazzie confirmed it to the press—that he couldn't decide whether to dunk the ball or lay it against the backboard. What occurred was a combination of the two which didn't work. Shortly thereafter De-Busschere blocked a shot and got the ball downcourt to Cazzie again. This time Russell stopped at the free-throw line and put in the line-drive jumper that has so endeared him to the fans.

The movement provided by Bradley and Frazier was a key element of last night's victory, particuarly in the first half. At the beginning of the season I noticed that Frazier tended to move the ball and Bradley seemed to encourage physical movement of the players by his own tireless picking, cutting, and screening. This was the case last night. In addition, the two teamed up for some fine defensive plays in the first quarter.

Mike Riordan certainly gets the guts award for the two plays he pulled off last night that were critical to the victory. In the first half, Riordan challenged Alcindor on a drive to the basket and outfaked him, avoiding the long arms and big hands that could have blocked his layup. In the fourth quarter, when the Knicks were fighting to overcome a Milwaukee lead that reached as much as 6 points, Riordan took Jon McGlocklin one-on-one. McGlockin played Mike perfectly, but Riordan improvised a wild—and successful—hook shot after penetrating to the foul lane. That basket provided tremendous impetus for the drive that overtook the Bucks.

Milwaukee now faces a rugged chore—they absolutely have to sweep the two games in Wisconsin on Friday night and Sunday afternoon. If the Knicks can come home with a split, they will have a 3–1 lead, needing only one victory to clinch the series with two games at home and one on the road to attempt it. On the other hand, should Milwaukee even the series, the Knicks will be in trouble. The broad spacing of the games so far, with four days of rest between

143

the second and third games, works to the Knicks' advantage. Willis Reed has a bad knee for which only cortisone and rest seem to do any good, with rest the best medicine of all. The third, fourth, and fifth games will be played over three days —Friday, Sunday, and Monday—a scheduling situation that seems to favor Milwaukee.

In the Western Division, the Lakers overtook and passed the Suns after trailing 3 games to 1, then opened their divisional final at Atlanta by trouncing the Hawks. Atlanta had opened up a 15-point lead at halftime, but the Lakers jammed the Hawks' running game and recovered to win. Either team would be extremely tough. The Hawks have outstanding size, strength, speed, and shooting. The Lakers seem only now to be discovering what a team with Baylor, West, and Chamberlain can do—and, should West and Baylor get as far as the finals, the fact that they have never won all the marbles could spur them to a superhuman effort. Hawks' coach Richie Guerin was fined $1,000 by Commissioner Kennedy for comments he made about the officiating following the Laker victory. The remarks included threats of bloodshed in the second game of the series and were, to say the least, intemperate.

Before the start of Saturday's game, the Garden crowd stood for a moment of silence in memory of Maurice Stokes, who died last week. Stokes was a star for the Cincinnati Royals in the late Fifties who suffered a brain injury as a result of a fall during a playoff game in 1958 and was paralyzed from then until his death. Jack Twyman, another former star of the Royals and now the color man on the ABC telecasts, became Stokes' official guardian, providing the money for extensive hospitalization and medical care through benefit games and other contributions. The story of Stokes' fight to overcome his paralysis and his good cheer through the years he was infirm is inspiring and heroically tragic. And the story of Twyman's voluntary guardianship and good will is noble. The fact that Stokes was black and Twyman is white is only meaningful in the context of American racial problems that should never have been. Sports has frequently been held up as a model for society, where a man's ability is the stick by which he is measured and where devotion to team must overcome ego. Even in sports, unfortunately, it frequently does not turn out quite that way, although it would be fair to say that sports is more faithful to these values than is society at large. Twyman's immediate and lasting assistance to a fellow human rendered incapable of caring for himself is a lesson that can do us all some good. During that moment of silence, my thoughts were of Jack Twyman as much as of Maurice Stokes. Just as they would be with any man who chooses to help carry another's burden.

APRIL 21

After the Knicks salvaged a split in Milwaukee and needed only to win at home last night to go into the NBA championship finals against Los Angeles, I had the strongest feeling I could remember that they would win the game. Early in the season, particularly in the midst of the eighteen-game streak, you went to the Garden to watch an exhibition of professional basketball—not to find out who was going to win. In early December, however, the Knicks became just another winning ballclub and the possibility of their losing was present at any game. I didn't feel that possibility before last night's game, and neither did any of the people I talked to who have been following the season.

Perhaps it was the nature of the two games at Milwaukee that created that feeling. The Knicks lost on Friday night,

101–96, in a game where Milwaukee opened several very large leads, only to see the Knicks storm back time after time. Lew Alcindor was magnificent in Friday's game, with 31 rebounds to go with his 33 points. The loss cut the series margin to 2–1 for New York, but even after Friday's game there seemed little to worry about. The reason the Knicks lost was not Alcindor, nor a good game by Freddy Crawford, nor a tight Milwaukee defense, although all were present in the game. The Knicks simply failed to hit shots they have to hit and *have* hit all season. They played solid defense, passed well, hit the open man, and penetrated for high-percentage shots. They just couldn't put the ball in the basket. In fact, the margin of 5 points could have been made up easily. Cazzie Russell, for the second game in a row, missed an unmolested layup on a fast break when he got caught between a dunk and a shot off the boards. Dave DeBusschere was 0-for-4 at the foul line, which is extremely unusual. To place the blame solely with DeBusschere and Russell, however, would be grossly unfair. All the Knicks, Dave and Cazzie included, played well in every facet of the game except putting the ball in the hoop. There is no question that the Knicks are the best-shooting team in the NBA—only Nate Bowman is *not* a top-notch outside shooting threat—and there was no doubt that if they could keep the rest of their game together, their shooting would recover sufficiently for victory.

So they attempted to demonstrate this on Sunday afternoon. This game was nationally televised, and the Knicks have a woeful record in nationally televised games, but they started as if they were going to show the nation what all the talk had been about. The starters opened a modest 29–23 advantage in the first quarter before the bench took over to run up a 65–45 halftime lead. The psychology of momentum was clearly demonstrated in the contrast between Friday night's game and Sunday's first half. When a team is missing, they start passing up shots that they should take, particularly medium-range jump shots of fifteen feet or so. When everybody is hitting, they take shots when they're open. The sooner a team takes an open shot, the less is the risk of losing the ball on a passing or dribbling error or a 24-second violation.

Despite the Knicks' big halftime lead, Milwaukee refused to quit. Led by Alcindor, they stormed back in the third quarter, at one time cutting the deficit to 69–67, an amazing run. Then Cazzie, Friday night's nominal goat, became Sunday's hero with a succession of jumpers that restored New York's offense and the Knicks began to move away again. The lead was only 82–79 at the end of the third quarter, but Reed and Frazier opened things up at the beginning of the fourth quarter and the Knicks won going away, 117–105.

I think the reason for the overwhelming confidence going into last night's game was that the Knicks had never really been intimidated or flustered by the Bucks in the first four games. Milwaukee did as well as it could on Friday night and still needed a horrendous shooting performance by New York to come up a winner. Reed, clearly, is not yet overmatched by Alcindor, although he may be in years to come as Lew gets stronger and more experienced. Frazier's defense had practically driven Flynn Robinson, Milwaukee's second-leading scorer and one of the best shooters in basketball, out of the series. On Friday night, Robinson lost his starting position to Fred Crawford. Robinson finally started again last night, but he played only 16 minutes.

From the start of last night's game, the Knicks left no doubt that the fans' confidence was not misplaced. Milwaukee led 4–0 in the opening minute, but by the end of the first quarter they were so clearly defeated that it was

147

all over. Dick Barnett nailed the lid in the Bucks' coffin with 9 points in the first 3 minutes of the game, including a 3-point play where he hit a 25-foot jumper despite being fouled hard on the shot. Barnett scored 16 points in the first quarter, pacing New York to a 35–19 lead before taking his usual rest. Subsequent to Barnett's flurry, which was probably the most exciting offensive quarter any Knick has had this season, Bill Bradley and Willis Reed got hot, helping to run the lead to 69–45 at the half. The final Milwaukee bucket of the first half came on a 50-foot hook shot by Guy Rodgers at the buzzer. Rodgers' impossible shot and a couple of flamboyant stuffs by Alcindor were all any Milwaukee fan might have had to cheer about as the Knicks continued to widen their lead throughout the second half. The final score was 132–96.

The exhibition that the Knicks put on last night was probably their strongest of the season, although I think some fans and writers who say this may be forgetting some pretty memorable games, particuarly one at Atlanta and an earlier victory over the Bucks at the Garden. In any case, there was little that could be improved upon. The passing was crisp and frequently dazzling as the Knicks threw chest passes, bounce passes, lob passes, and passes around their backs and over their shoulders to get layups on fast breaks and set plays. The defense gave the Bucks no peace as Frazier and Bradley, particularly, swooped in on Buck ballhandlers to make a steal to key a fast break. Though Milwaukee led in the final rebound statistics, the Knicks cannot be faulted on the boards, either. With Alcindor frequently forced to shoot jumpers from the baseline by the impenetrable Reed, the Bucks were frequently limited to one shot—when indeed they could get a shot at all.

The fans really appreciated the show. The starters were removed from the game one by one, and each got a standing ovation. The loudest and longest cheer was for Willis Reed, who received a standing ovation that lasted through several minutes of action after his removal. Willis never did stand up to acknowledge the cheers of the crowd, but when he stood to congratulate Dave DeBusschere when Dave came out, the crowd cheered even louder, as if Reed were rising to respond to the cheers. Bill Hosket failed to get into the game because of an ankle injury he sustained in practice. When the explanation of his continued presence on the bench was made over the public-address system during a Knick time-out, the crowd rose again in a good-natured ovation for Hosket. Bill raised an outstretched fist to show his appreciation and the crowd roared louder.

For all the heartwarming crowd reactions as the Knicks wrapped up Phase Two of the playoffs, there was an extremely disturbing element of crowd response. I discovered it early in the first quarter when four young men in business suits behind me started a nonstop diatribe at Alcindor, screaming pointless insults at the top of their lungs. This type of thing is unusual among Knick fans. There is booing directed at the opposition and at the officials, but I had never heard the kind of psychotic rudeness to an opposing player that these men exhibited. It finally got the best of me and I turned around.

"Aside from being really loud, all the screaming at Alcindor that you're doing is bush, just plain bush. Why don't you go to some small town to do that stuff?"

At first these guys were totally taken aback by my criticism. It slowed them down for a couple of minutes, but then they started again, louder than before, and probably with the intention of hassling me as much as they could ever hassle Alcindor. After some stage whispers about my having made the comment to them, I turned around to repeat it. That, it was obviously made clear to me, was a

149

mistake. Any group of morons stupid and boorish enough to scream the kind of insults they were screaming would obviously fight for their right to do so without criticism. And I do mean fight. And I do mean without criticism. I felt like the silent majority was breathing down my back, and all the hair on my head couldn't keep that uncomfortable hot air off my neck.

The confrontation could have become even more unpleasant and even, I thought, physically dangerous, so I studiously avoided turning around again. Alcindor's tormentors (or should I say "my tormentors") seemed to run out of gas until a combination of kids and what Thomas Rogers of *The New York Times* guesses are New York Giant fans started singing "Good-bye, Lewie, we hate to see you go" from the balcony after Alcindor was removed near the end of the third quarter. I would hate to hazard a guess as to how many of the 19,500 fans in the Garden participated in the only shameful display of bad sportsmanship that has occurred at a Knick home game all year, but the four fellows in back of me were among them.

The chanting died down soon enough; the Knicks' play, even with an insurmountable lead, attracted enough attention so that there was little left for chanting. Nonetheless, in today's *Times* there was an entire half-column article about the Alcindor criticism stating that the Knicks were "perplexed and vaguely embarrassed" by it.

As far as I had noticed during the season, the noisy idiots behind me had never been in those seats before. A great number of the regulars in Section 111 were not around for last night's game, partly because of the Passover holiday.

Los Angeles beat Atlanta in four-straight games, so it will be the Lakers and the Knicks in the final four-of-seven clash beginning this Friday night at the Garden. The Lakers have now won seven-straight playoff games, and the Knicks

150

will be facing a red-hot team. It is hard to figure exactly how the Laker series will go. When Chamberlain got hurt last November, Los Angeles speeded up their attack to give West and Baylor a chance to do their magic before the opposition defense was set. With Chamberlain to set picks outside and to screen and score in deep, Los Angeles has returned to the more deliberate style that has characterized their play since they obtained him. They are extremely talented and the injuries they suffered gave playing time to a lot of players now on the bench, so the Lakers can match even New York's depth. The Lakers are in the NBA finals for the seventh time in the past ten years and nobody could want to win the championship more than the oft-frustrated West and Baylor. If the Knicks are to win, they will have to run hard on the Lakers and force them to play at an unaccustomed quicker pace. With a healthy Chamberlain, Los Angeles may be the toughest opponent the Knicks have faced since they beat the Lakers with Chamberlain, 99–96, on the first Saturday night of the season. It is safe to assume that the finals will go at least six games, and quite likely the limit of seven. If the Knicks can maintain the brilliance they exhibited against Milwaukee, they will win. Anything less than that and it will be a real dogfight. The NBA championship that has been dangling like the proverbial carrot before New York's eyes since last October is finally close enough to be snatched.

APRIL 26

The regulars were all in their seats in Section 111 before the tip-off of the opening game of the championship series on Friday night—the Knicks against the complete, unabridged edition of the Los Angeles Lakers. For the first time in calendar year 1970 the fellow who sits in front of me arrived *before* the National Anthem was played. The four rabid fans behind me had returned to their posts after missing the Buck final because of Passover. The sentiment was overwhelming: "I wouldn't miss this series for anything." I heard that our $12.50 seats were worth at least $50 outside, despite the fact that Madison Square Garden had opened up an extra few thousand seats at $6 in the Felt Forum where the game was on close-circuit television.

Back in October (just pages from your front cover), Los Angeles had come to town for the first Saturday night game of the season. Then, as now, they sported Chamberlain, Baylor, and West, but the Knicks had not seen the three together since then, even though they had played the Lakers five times in the interim. That October game was, I remember, like a playoff game, and the season was only barely underway. What made that game reminiscent of classic playoff action was the tenacity of both teams: they had both fought back from deficits, and both had played brilliant ball. The Knicks won that one, 99–96—and in a somewhat similar struggle, took a 1–0 lead in the playoff finals on Friday, 124–112.

The big question on the minds of the Professional Basketball Watchers was how well Willis Reed would fare against Wilt Chamberlain. Chamberlain's restored health had revitalized the entire Laker ballclub. As expected, Reed went outside on Chamberlain from the very start, attempting to force Wilt to play farther away from the boards. What must have been pleasantly surprising to Knick fans, however, was the extent of Reed's success outside. Shooting mostly from 15-to-20 feet range, Reed hit on 7 of his first 9 shots on his way to a 25-point first half. His outside shooting ability made the Knicks' whole ballgame work. When Chamberlain came away from the boards, the picks that Willis set

152

for DeBusschere and Bradley were made that much more effective. When they came off them they could drive inside without running into the specter of a 7-foot-2 giant to swat away their layups, and Willis was able to roll for some flashy dunk shots as he beat Chamberlain in the 15-foot race to the board. What was expected—but a necessary part of the Knicks' strategy—was that Reed would beat Chamberlain downcourt after the Lakers' offense terminated time after time. Primarily on the strength of their advantage at center, the Knicks raced to a 50–30 lead before half the second quarter was over.

The Lakers, however, have the firepower, experience, poise, and depth to fight back from large deficits. Boston had a mammoth lead in the final game of the championship round last Spring and the Lakers stormed back to put the Celtics on the ropes at the buzzer, although Bill Russell and his men held on for their eleventh championship. The Knicks' problem in stopping a Laker comeback was that nobody could stop Jerry West. Walt Frazier picked up three personals fairly early in the second quarter making the attempt, but by halftime the Lakers had clawed to within 11 points, 65–54. Riordan was playing well in relief of the starters, but both Dave Stallworth and Cazzie Russell had their problems in the second quarter. Russell, particularly, couldn't get untracked. He missed a couple of shots and then bungled the interception of a long downcourt pass by the Lakers that allowed Happy Hairston to score at the buzzer.

The third quarter was all Los Angeles. Earlier in the season, the third quarter was frequently when the Knicks asserted their superiority and wrapped up ballgames. The explanation for this was simple: the starters were getting a rest during the second quarter while the opposition starters were still playing, so the Knick first-string, fresh and rested,

153

would be just overwhelming to start the second half. But in the playoffs this had not been true—not in the Baltimore series nor in the Milwaukee series. Milwaukee, particularly, cut a substantial Knickerbocker halftime lead to nothing during the fourth game of the Eastern Division finals.

The Lakers did better than that. With Reed missing shots he'd been hitting during his torrid first half, and DeBusschere and Bradley being outmanned on the boards, Los Angeles stormed into the lead by the end of the quarter, 92–89. The *News* writer indicated that he felt extremely worried at about that time and that the fans were concerned, but I did not detect that feeling around me. The Knicks were not playing badly. It was simply that their shots were not dropping. This happened to them in the ballgame they lost at Milwaukee the previous Friday night, but no serious observer of the Knicks can expect medium-range outside shooting to be their problem too often. Surely enough, they started to click again in the fourth quarter— after the Lakers had scored to stretch their lead to 5 points —and the Knicks won going away.

Cazzie certainly redeemed himself in the second half. He went in for Bill Bradley, who had hit three nice jump shots in the third quarter to help keep the Knicks in the game, and Russell was as tough as you like him. He hit three very big jumps and a drive down the stretch to help supply the Knick momentum and continued playing the improved defense he had shown against the Bucks. Mike Riordan also played extremely well during the fourth quarter, scoring a healthy share of his 19 points near the finish. Reed also found the range again to pop home a few more and finish with 37 points, 4 better than West and high for both teams. Both Russell and Riordan challenged Chamberlain on drives and scored, leading to widespread conjecture that Wilt, recovered or not, can't jump like he used

154

to. "They caught me flatfooted," was Chamberlain's comment.

Even Max admitted on Friday night that Riordan "has improved 500 percent during the playoffs." I think it's just that Max is noticing. Riordan has steadily improved from the beginning of the season, and the confidence he is getting from each better ballgame just serves as a catalyst for further improvement. He no longer hesitates to drive in important situations, nor does he look to pass up a long jumper when he finds himself open. He has continued, as his point-making has increased, to play tenacious defense and to help on the boards the way he always has. Part of Barnett's recent outpouring of points must be attributed to Riordan's improvement. No team can use the guard assigned to Riordan to help on Barnett when the two are playing together.

Walt Frazier's point production continued to be low—he took only five shots against L.A. and scored only 6 points—but his play is as sparkling and important as it has ever been. West scored heavily on Frazier while Walt was guarding him during the first half, but Frazier's tactic of making West work from baseline to baseline to get himself open eventually took its toll. While Walt was shackled with some foul trouble, Barnett took over the chore of guarding the tiring West and practically shut him out as the teams came down the stretch. The end moments of important ballgames are usually Jerry West's moments, but not on Friday night.

Two sets of honors were monopolized by the Knicks last week, but one received considerably more attention than the other. The less-publicized news was Holzman's selection as NBA Coach of the Year. Red received seventeen votes to nine for his closest pursuer, and no honor was ever more deserved. The testimonies to Holzman's ability as a head man are not just in the team's record but—in a much larger sense—in the way the victories are achieved. The Knicks are prepared to do the right thing, night after night, such as the way they set up Reed for perimeter jumpers at the outset of the Laker game. Mike Riordan's improvement from a fringe NBA ballplayer to a reliable stalwart has to be a credit to Holzman as well as Riordan. And the fact that the men on the bench are ready attests to the healthy attitude Holzman has maintained even among players who see little action.

What seemed to excite the fans and press more than Holzman's recognition was the fact that three Knickerbockers were named to the all-NBA defensive team. Walt Frazier led the balloting, with 27 out of a possible 28 votes, as the top defensive guard in the league. Willis Reed was named at center, and Dave DeBusschere was the top defensive forward. Gus Johnson of Baltimore and Jerry West rounded out the team. It is certainly true that the individual honors were deserved, but the defensive work of Dick Barnett, Bill Bradley, and Mike Riordan throughout the season and through the playoffs is certainly not lost on the Knick fans. If the key to the Knick success—properly characterized in virtually every newspaper and magazine article written on them—is teamwork, then the team defense is the outstanding manifestation of that key.

Sometime during the Baltimore series, the fans started chanting "Defense! Defense! Defense!" during key moments of ballgames. The Knicks have certainly popularized an important element of basketball that heretofore had not been appreciated nearly as much as the time-honored ability to put the ball in the hoop. You get the feeling that any Knick fan would rather see a clean steal than a driving layup, and there are few sets of fans that feel that way in any sport. A home run has always been more exciting than a strikeout, a touchdown pass of more interest than a tackle. If the

Knicks have accomplished nothing else this year, they have gained recognition for an overlooked area of sport.

It is certainly better to be up a game than down one, but the Laker series has a long way to go. Reed suffered a shoulder injury during the first half on Friday night, which may have affected his shooting after the intermission—and may hamper his effectiveness when the series resumes at the Garden tomorrow. The Knicks have taken the Lakers' good punch—33 points by West, 21 by Baylor, 24 rebounds by Chamberlain—and won. If the Knicks can maintain the pace they have set, there seems to be little Los Angeles can do to stop them from taking the championship. The slightest slip by New York, however, particularly on outside shooting and defense, will put them in serious trouble. Should the Knicks win the second game, Los Angeles will have its back to the wall. But if the performance slips and the Lakers can even things up, they will be going home in good shape to take command. The Knicks' performance in the opener indicates: "We've gotten this far, let's not blow it now."

Amen.

APRIL 29

When you lose a ballgame by 105–103, as the Knicks did to the Lakers on Monday night, you can always cite several "if" factors. If Mike Riordan had not thrown away a couple of passes, the Knicks might have won. If Dick Barnett had hit the jump shot he took with 3 seconds left, the Knicks might have won. If a three-for-two foul attempt by Walt Frazier had not been called back by a Laker 24-second violation, the Knicks might have won. If Willis Reed's first-half basket that was nullified because he stepped on the baseline coming around the pick had counted, the Knicks might have won. And, perhaps, if the Knicks had called

time-out with 8 seconds to go in the game when they regained possession from Los Angeles, they might have won.

But the final score was Lakers 105, Knicks 103. And you
know whom I blame? Not Riordan for throwing away passes.
Not officials Rush and Powers, despite an extremely questionable 3-second call on Dave Stallworth near the end of
the game to go with the calls on Frazier and Reed. Not
even Dick Barnett, for missing the crucial jumper. I blame
whoever the idiot is who designed the scoreboards in Madison Square Garden. If the Knicks lose the championship to
Los Angeles, this guy ought to be drowned in the cham-
pagne the Knicks might otherwise have been drinking.

Picture the situation: The Lakers' Dick Garrett throws
the ball away near midcourt. The Knicks intercept and Dick
Barnett is driving down the left side of the floor, with
Garrett in hot pursuit. Dave Stallworth and Keith Erickson,
a Knick and a Laker, are ahead of the play. Barnett knows
the Knicks need a basket to tie it up. How much time does
he have to shoot it? How would he ever know? The scoreboard clocks at Madison Square Garden are located high
above and far behind the baskets. And the numbers on the
scoreboards are not big, bold numbers. You'd have to look
hard to find them. Dick Barnett never had enough time to
look. It could have taken a half-hour to find the numbers
on that scoreboard, and he had only 3 seconds.

With those 3 seconds to use, Barnett might have scored,
or at least been fouled. The odds are on it. But not knowing
how much time was left, he hurried a shot that was slightly
beyond his best range. The odds are against it. The Knicks
lose.

New York just couldn't quite put it together for a long
enough time to put the game away on Monday night. De-
Busschere couldn't hit a shot in the first half, and the bench
lacked firepower. But the starters provided a late spurt that
pulled the Knicks even at intermission. Los Angeles pulled

out again during the third quarter, but the Knicks again caught up.

Tied at 81 at the end of the third quarter, I asked everybody around me if they were nervous. It seemed everybody but me was. My error. When the Knicks made a couple of quick steals and fancy passes to start the fourth quarter, I was about to pat my own back for *knowing* they'd pull it out. I forgot about Jerry West and Wilt Chamberlain.

West just about fouled out the whole Knick backcourt. Walt Frazier picked up his fifth with 9 minutes to go in the game. A 6-minute "rest" for Frazier obviously didn't help the Knicks any. Barnett finished with five personals and Riordan had two in 15 minutes of play. West shot fifteen fouls. He was off, hitting only ten, which would have been an "if" for the Lakers if the score had been reversed at the end. It wasn't, because ten was enough. The last two were points 104 and 105.

The game was a peculiar one. The Knicks outrebounded the Lakers by a substantial margin, 59–46, and took ten more shots. Without a statistic sheet in front of me, I am willing to bet that the Knicks didn't lose another ballgame all year where they had the rebounding edge *and* the shot-attempt edge. In the second half the outside shooting was strong and they still couldn't pull it out.

One reason has to be Wilt Chamberlain. Wilt matched the 24 rebounds he had in the first game but was considerably more effective. He clogged the middle, blocking drives and switching quickly on defense. He harassed Willis into a 12-for-29 shooting performance from the floor. And when the Lakers needed points, Wilt went to the basket.

The net result of the whole thing is that the Knicks have to get a split in Los Angeles. They must win tonight. Failing that, they absolutely must win on Friday night. There is no particular reason why they should not, but there is no detectable reason why they should have lost Monday night's game.

I must be a fan of unmitigated faith, in common sense if not in the Knicks. Common sense tells me that the Knicks are a better team than the Lakers and that they outplayed them during those first two games. Common sense says that somebody besides Willis Reed is going to get a hot hand for the Knicks in this series, and the Lakers couldn't withstand that. Common sense reminds me that Chamberlain and West have played more minutes than anybody in this series and that has to take a toll.

Bill Bradley is quoted as saying that the Los Angeles Forum offers the least disadvantage to the visiting team of any arena in the NBA. The fans' lack of enthusiasm, despite their number, doesn't provide the Lakers much of a "home-court advantage."

Through it all the eternal optimist, I still think the Knicks will win this thing—in six games at most. I thought it would go longer, but the more I think about Monday night's game the more I knew the Knicks couldn't have lost it.

Both the Knicks and the Lakers are trying for their first NBA crown with the idea that this may be the last year they can win it. Milwaukee's acquisition of Oscar Robertson, teaming the best passer in basketball history with Lew Alcindor, bodes the birth of a new dynasty. So say many experts. And it just may be that they are right. It just may be that 1970 is the worst year an NBA team could ever choose to say "Wait 'til next year." Unless that team is the Milwaukee Bucks.

MAY 2

It is always difficult to put the present into proper perspective, so it may very well be that the current Knick–

Laker series is not the most exciting in basketball history. But it would have to be tied with whatever was previously most exciting, because to exceed these four games in excitement, individual brilliance, and/or closeness would be impossible.

The Knicks split in Los Angeles, as the Lakers had done in New York, but they were awfully lucky to have done so. You could put it another way and say the Lakers were lucky not to be down 3–1 going back to New York. When two overtime games in a row have been played, I guess it is reasonable that each team should have won one, but the standoff in the won–lost columns only scratches the surface of the story.

Los Angeles knew they had to win on Wednesday night, having split in New York. The Lakers had gained the "home-court advantage" by winning the second game at the Garden, and their best hope of winning the series, according to all observers, was to maintain that advantage by winning in Los Angeles. So the Lakers charged out to do what they had to do. The Knicks were demolished as they had not been all year—with the Lakers rolling to a 56–42 halftime lead. The key to the Laker success, as usual, was fine shooting by Jerry West, but he was getting able assistance from Chamberlain on the boards and Keith Erickson on offense. Erickson was giving Bill Bradley fits, driving well and hitting perimeter jump shots when Bradley sagged in on Chamberlain, as per the Knicks' strategy to keep the big man from getting the ball in close. Los Angeles had kept the momentum they had gained in their second-game win in New York.

But the Knicks refused to give up. The defense pulled itself together in the third quarter. Dave DeBusschere and Dick Barnett, who hadn't been hitting in the first half, chipped 9 points off the Laker lead.

As the fourth quarter started, L.A. tried to reassert itself and had some early success, but Walt Frazier started roaming around, playing his sniping defense, and the Knicks' outside shots continued to drop. In the closing minutes, New York took the lead for the first time since early in the first quarter and Los Angeles stood to have a great first half wasted. The Knicks had the last shot with the game knotted at 100—or so they thought when Dave DeBusschere hit from the top of the key to give them a 2-point lead with 3 seconds left and the Lakers out of times-out.

Wilt Chamberlain, realizing the futility of the situation, caught DeBusschere's shot as it fell through, stepped back, and threw the ball out to Jerry West as most of the players headed off the court. West refused to concede. With only Willis Reed hassling him, West took a couple of dribbles up the middle and then cast a shot from about 10 feet behind the midcourt stripe. The ball fell through cleanly as the horn was sounding and players had to be fetched from the trail to the locker room to play a 5-minute overtime.

West's breathtaking shot, however, could not save the Lakers. New York hardly missed a shot in the overtime period and Dick Barnett hit a jumper with 3 seconds left to give the Knicks a 3-point lead, 111–108. Even Jerry West could do nothing about that—the Knicks were not about to give up a 3-point play. The series was now in New York's favor, 2–1, and everybody thought it was all over, except for the shouting. Certainly the disappointment of wasting a great first half and a nearly impossible effort by West would cast a psychological shadow on Los Angeles that would preclude their making up a 2–1 deficit in games.

The Knicks pressed their advantage as the fourth game opened last night. Dick Barnett gave the Laker defense

162

no peace, as he canned five consecutive jump shots in the first quarter to get the Knicks rolling. Still, L.A. refused to yield. Chamberlain was ineffective in the first quarter, but Elgin Baylor was doing a great job on the boards and teamed with West to bring the Lakers to within 3 points, 27–24, at the end of the first quarter.

The second quarter was all Lakers, with the Knick bench again failing to provide a lift. West was supposed to be hurting—his left thumb was jammed in the third game and he had been listed as a "doubtful starter," but it didn't seem to affect his shooting and ballhandling at all. He spearheaded the Laker drive, enhanced by substitutes Roberson and Egan as the Knicks had a page stolen from their own book. By halftime the Laker lead was 54–47, and it was only that small because the Knicks managed a baby spurt as the second quarter came to a close.

Impossible though it may seem, the Knicks again fought back in the second half. DeBusschere and Barnett were again the reliable shooters, and Willis Reed also began to get himself untracked. Los Angeles was working the ball inside to Chamberlain more and he was keeping the Lakers in points, but New York had whittled down the margin to 71–67 as the fourth quarter began.

And the fourth quarter was a rerun, almost. Again New York got a chance at the critical last shot, with the score tied 99–99. Frazier was looking for DeBusschere or Bradley, but neither could get open so Walt was forced to take the shot himself. Erickson applied heavy pressure on his jumper and the ball bounced off the front rim to send the two tired teams into their second-consecutive overtime.

This time Los Angeles was not to be denied. DeBusschere fouled out in the extra session, but in any case the Lakers were going to win this game. Elgin Baylor hit the critical basket, and John Tresvant came off the bench to ride the boards and hawk the ball for Los Angeles, and the Knicks never had a chance. The final score was 121–115—with an extremely high total of 38 points scored in the 5-minute overtime—and the series was squared, 2–2.

The television cameras had panned on the players of both teams during the playing of the Anthem before that game and what they showed was quite revealing. The Knicks were loose, burning off a little nervous energy during the Anthem, obviously anxious to get the game under way. The Lakers were very somber and pensive. Most of them were looking down at the floor, thinking very hard about the game coming up, which they absolutely had to win. The first 6 minutes of the game was an extension of the players' appearances before it started. The loose and ready Knicks jumped off to an 18–10 lead and looked for all the world like they would run the Lakers into the Pacific. Los Angeles was deliberate, and often uncertain, as they missed good shots and failed on the boards. But the momentum of the game shifted several times, and the Lakers controlled it enough to win.

West's performance in the fourth game—his heroics in all the previous games notwithstanding—was one of the amazing outputs any guard has ever produced. Despite the handicap of a sore left hand, which cut down on his mobility to the left, West hit 13-for-26 from the floor, 11-for-12 from the line, pulled in five rebounds, and handed off an incredible eighteen assists. There was nothing wrong with the defense that Dick Barnett played on West; he is simply unstoppable when he is hitting. And in this series he has been hitting.

Frazier, freed of the defensive assignment of guarding West, has picked up his ballhawking and his scoring. Walt

164

scored well in the two games in Los Angeles, after having sacrificed his shooting to an intolerable extent through the first two games of the series. Frazier averaged over 20 points a game during the regular season, and while the balance of the Knicks allows him to score less and defense more, a severe drop-off from the second-leading point-producer would hurt any club.

Mike Riordan has not played well in the Los Angeles series since the first game. Bill Bradley's shooting has been hot and cold, and Cazzie Russell and Dave Stallworth have yet to have a top game against L.A. The Lakers seem to be getting the best possible performance out of everyone. West has been superb, Baylor and Chamberlain have done their jobs. Keith Erickson has played better in the playoffs than he did against the Knicks all season, and Johnny Egan and Dick Garrett have frequently taken advantage of the double-teaming of West to hit open jump shots.

Both teams go into the fifth game of the series, in New York, feeling they "must win." This is more true for the Knicks. They must not allow Los Angeles the opportunity to wrap up the series in Los Angeles, which would be possible if the Lakers win. Willis Reed's knees are aching—a fact that certainly affected his play in the fourth game—but the Knicks must overcome this and any other problems, real or imagined, to keep the odd-game advantage. At no time during the playoffs have the Knicks trailed in games: Baltimore had them knotted at 2–2 and 3–3 and the Lakers have squared matters at 1–1 and 2–2.

In a sense, it is difficult to root against Los Angeles, except for the staunchest Knick fans. Wilt Chamberlain has shed his role of an ogre; Baylor and West have been two of the most popular basketball players around the league for years. Baylor and West, though often competing in the final round of the NBA playoffs, have never won a championship. There are some players who have failed to win championships who have been branded "losers"—both Oscar Robertson and Chamberlain have been so tagged from time to time. Neither Baylor nor West could ever be mentioned in this vein. Both are magnificent competitors when the chips are down—West particularly has been noted as "Mr. Clutch." They have always lost because of the strength of external forces—sometimes injuries, sometimes Bill Russell, sometimes an "impossible" shot by a Bob Cousy or a Sam Jones.

On the other hand, this is no time for Knick fans or Knick players to sentimentalize the Laker situation. With Oscar Robertson teaming with Lew Alcindor next year at Milwaukee, this is the best opportunity there will ever be to complete a Knickerbocker Year.

Perhaps what has made this such a fantastic series so far is the fact that both teams want the championship very badly. Some would say that the team that wants it most will win. But not in this series. Desire is a flat-footed tie. Unfortunately, a basketball game cannot end in a tie. Neither will this series.

MAY 6

There are no words. Reams of columns have been written. The sports segments of news reports have tried to explain it with words and pictures. They have all failed to communicate what happened on Monday night.

It was the triumph of intellect, the epitome of courage in the face of adversity. It was the ultimate communal experience. It was the most captivating theater—although it would have been unbelievable on any stage but a basketball court. It was a premature climax that was completely gratifying.

It was the Knicks. Completely, undeniably, lovably—only

the Knicks. No other team could have done what they did—not this year, not ever. It was the 200-pound muscleman turned quickly into a 97-pound weakling—but winning anyway.

All the pregame talk was about the condition of Willis Reed. Now he had two aching knees, not just one. The Knicks needed their irreplaceable giant to struggle through two more victories—else how would they bring home the bacon?

I was there early to see every pregame layup, and my eyes buttressed my fears. Willis was limping. Willis was hurting. He could not run without pain. He could not jump without a grimace. But he would play. He would try.

The Lakers were as merciless as they had to be. They wanted the same bacon. They kept working the ball in to Wilt Chamberlain, starting from the first offensive series. They would test Willis, push him, make him work and strain. It was only the first quarter, and the Knicks already trailed by 10 points.

With about 5 minutes to go in the opening stanza, Reed got the ball at the high post. He looked for the foul-line jump shot that Chamberlain had conceded him throughout the playoffs. He looked for his eighth and ninth points, although only he knew the pain that he inflicted upon himself in scoring his first seven. He had to score because he couldn't jump. He had no rebounds.

Chamberlain would not concede the jumper this time. He came out and Willis went around him. Willis had room to his left—his strong driving side—and he had that step he needed.

Then, with the suddenness of a gunshot, Willis was down, looking helplessly from the floor as the Lakers picked up the loose ball and stormed to the other end, Chamberlain leading the way. Dave DeBusschere tied up Wilt for a jump ball

167

at the Lakers' foul circle, but few fans saw that. None of the photographers did. Restrained by the baseline as if by a barbed-wire fence, the photographers recorded the fall of the Knickerbockers. Tomorrow the captions would read —"This is what a season looks like when it is sitting on the floor."

The jump ball gives Danny Whelan time to help Willis to his feet, and though we all know he cannot play, Willis tries to continue. A few more seconds of playing time elapses and Willis cannot push his body anymore. Nate Bowman goes in for him as tears well in the eyes of all the women around me, and some of the men. So it has come to this. We have followed the Knicks for so long, and from time to time we felt the fates might deny us a championship. And this is the way it happens.

The Knicks were disorganized and visibly upset. Frazier and Bradley ran and hawked and stole the ball. But nobody could put it in the hoop. Bowman could not handle Chamberlain, so Bill Hosket tried. Hosket could not hit the shots from the outside that must go in if Wilt is to be pulled away from the boards. Willis Reed hits those shots.

Miraculously, the Knicks trailed by only 13 points at halftime, 53–40. Enough miracles! Chamberlain had 18 points already. Who would stop him from getting 30 more in the second half? In Section 111, and undoubtedly in every other section of the Garden, we sat and plotted. What could Holzman do? We nurtured ideas and then discarded them. "There is no rational way that we can expect the Knicks to win the game." That's what I said at halftime.

There's a new lineup for the second half. Dave DeBusschere is at center at 6-foot-6, giving away 8 big inches to Chamberlain—and who knows how many pounds? Bill Bradley and Cazzie Russell are at forward, both 6-foot-5. Frazier and Barnett are at guard, both 6-foot-4. To stop

Jerry West? And Wilt Chamberlain? And Elgin Baylor? When they were already 13 points ahead in a game they wanted so badly to win?

With confidence and fluidity, the Lakers took the tap, working a play based on the knowledge that Chamberlain could win it and tap it wherever they wanted it to go. There were so many people milling in the aisles that I thought people were starting to leave. If Willis can't play Wednesday, I thought, then this it for the season. The Knicks won't be home again.

We all thought our thoughts, but we all tried to help. The noise level kept going up and up, until it couldn't get any louder. But it did. The Knicks were pressing with their little men, trying hard. The minutes were ticking by and the Lakers could not expand that lead. Indeed, it was diminishing slightly, but the Knicks couldn't hit the shot that would put them really close. DeBusschere was leaning on Chamberlain the way he had on Gus Johnson, straining every muscle to keep the big man away from the boards. It was working, and yet victory remained inconceivable.

But those dead-eye shooters were starting to hit now. DeBusschere was playing well out in the corner on the 1–3–1 offense the Knicks employed. Chamberlain wouldn't go out to get him, so he fired a jumper and scored. Once again, twice again, Chamberlain would not leave that station near the basket and risk losing the rebound to harass the shooter. So he was right there to catch the ball as it fell through the net.

Finally, Wilt concedes. He must go out on DeBusschere. Bill Bradley, who is credited with suggesting the 1–3–1 to Holzman, cuts down the empty lane from the high post and DeBusschere whips the ball by Chamberlain. Bradley's layup is uncontested.

Dick Barnett is playing his heart out. Jerry West is having

169

fits, baseline to baseline, as Barnett gives him no peace. On a crucial play, the Knicks lose the ball to Mel Counts, a 7-foot forward. Barnett anticipates Counts' move and draws an important offensive foul. The Knicks' score increases by two.

At the end of the third quarter the Knicks trail by only 82–75. Almost half of the halftime deficit has been made up. Still so far to go. DeBusschere is in foul trouble, and the fourth quarter is Jerry West time. You feel in your heart that they might be able to do it, but then you know that they cannot. They have done so much already, and there is still so far to go.

The Lakers score to open the fourth quarter and their lead is back up to 9 points. There will be no concession by the Knicks, however. The press continues, forcing turnovers in backcourt, sniping passes in forecourt. Then De-Busschere's string runs out and he picks up his fifth personal foul.

Dave Stallworth comes in, and now he must guard Chamberlain. He cannot do it in the same way DeBusschere has. No Knickerbocker—save Willis Reed—is as strong as DeBusschere. Stallworth must use speed. He must substitute speed and cunning for height and weight. So Stallworth hides behind Chamberlain, jumping out on either side of him to prevent passes into the low post. He slaps a couple away, steals one to start a successful fast break.

The Knicks get one shot and one shot only. When they fail to hit, the Lakers get the ball. Frazier substitutes a steal for a rebound. Jerry West brings the ball up the middle of the floor, slowing things up and rallying his troops. Clyde flicks his wrist and West is now watching Frazier score on a layup.

Stallworth cannot, usually, shoot as well as DeBusschere, but sometimes he gets hot. Now he bombs a couple over

Chamberlain. When Wilt comes out, Stallworth drives and makes an "impossible" reverse layup that might have taught Elgin Baylor something. In any case, Baylor couldn't stop it.

Bradley hits the jump shot from the top of the key that ties the game at 87 and the Garden explodes. With over 7 minutes to go, it is a question of sustaining momentum, not of time. With a little over 5 minutes to go, Bradley hits a carbon-copy jumper and the Knicks take the lead, 95–93. There is no doubt anymore, and the final score is 107–100.

The euphoria of the fifth-game triumph has not yet worn off, but the Knicks face the stern challenge again tonight. Willis is in Los Angeles for the sixth game, but it is doubtful that he will play. It was not his knee that gave out on him when he had gone down. He had slipped and bruised a couple of muscles in his hip. The pain is still severe and neither Holzman nor Whelan will allow Reed to risk a career for one ballgame. Beside, if the Knicks cannot repeat their Reed-less miracle tonight in Los Angeles, they will likely have him back for the seventh game at the Garden on Friday night. His knees will have had that much rest. Perhaps his hip will recover.

In the long run, the most important aspect of the fifth game might be the play of Cazzie Russell. It is dangerous to base conclusions on one game, but it surely looked like Cazzie can play defense and move the ball quickly on offense if he wants to badly enough. Of course, Cazzie scored well—he was 8-for-14 from the floor with 20 points—but he also led the Knicks in rebounds with eight and assisted in forcing several Laker turnovers.

The Knicks beat the Lakers by using an offense without a specialist. Frazier and Bradley did a little more passing, Russell, Barnett, and DeBusschere or Stallworth a little more shooting, but the 1–3–1 worked because all five men on the

171

court could shoot from the outside, dribble, pass, and drive. The Lakers were forced to guard each man tightly and honestly, one-on-one, and the Knick cutters broke quickly and the Knick ballhandlers took advantage of the wide-open spaces.

On defense, the Knicks moved like lightning. Barnett shut West off—Jerry did not score from the floor in the second half—with much less help than usual, for the emphasis was on keeping the ball from Chamberlain. The Knick defense did well in "hiding" the Laker's open man—always important when the defense double-teams—on the other side of the court from the ball. The Lakers could not move the ball to the open spot as quickly as the small Knicks could move their bodies, and the tempo was completely in New York's hands.

The *Post's* early edition carries no betting line on tonight's game, probably because of Reed's expected absence. It would seem that the miracle of Monday night cannot be repeated away from home with the Lakers having time to prepare for it and adjust. Holzman, apparently realizing that the element of surprise was crucial to the success of his "midget" lineup, does not plan to try it again. Nate Bowman will start at center (if Reed does not play) and the Knicks will return to a more conventional style. If the Lakers win tonight, and if Willis is not in top form on Friday, the Knicks' backs are no further from the wall than they have ever been. Regardless of what happens from here on in, the Knicks have provided one of the most amazing moments in sports history. If the Mets were Destiny's Darlings, the Knicks seem to be her child, and any prediction of what is to come based on what has passed is pointless and anti-climactic. We knew only that we must expect a surprise ending.

MAY 8

Wednesday night's game was a nightmare. I don't think there is another word that can describe it accurately. Willis, as expected, could not play, and Holzman started with Nate Bowman at center, fully realizing that his "no-center" alignment (as it has come to be called in the local press) could not work for 48 minutes. The short team depends on surprise, on quick switching of the tempo. It is unreasonable to assume that Dave Stallworth or Dave DeBusschere, regardless of the extent of their assistance, can keep Wilt Chamberlain from getting the ball for 48 minutes. With the height advantage Chamberlain has against Stallworth and DeBusschere, he needs only to get the ball to score.

Chamberlain had no trouble with Bowman, either. Wilt scored 45 points for the Lakers on Wednesday night and a great number of them came in the first quarter, when Los Angeles jumped into a 36–16 lead. The Knicks played them almost even for the rest of the game, at times going to the "no-center" lineup, but mostly playing Bowman at center. The final score was 135–113.

The Knicks were not as sharp as they were on Monday night. At times they seemed ready to make a meaningful run at Los Angeles, despite the fact that their 20-point deficit remained at halftime. In the fourth quarter, particularly, things were looking up for a time. With more than 8 minutes to go, the Knicks climbed to within 13 points, 107–94. A flurry of Laker turnovers and missed shots followed, but the Knicks could not capitalize to hit the basket or two that would have sustained their momentum and forced the Lakers to recall Monday night. When the ice broke on the teams' sloppy spell, it was West who broke it for Los Angeles.

So now the entire season rests on one ballgame, tonight's. The newspapers and radio reports indicate that Willis's chances of playing are 50/50 or better. Those are his chances of playing. He will play if he can move, and the doctors think there is little chance of reinjury. But nobody talks about how *well* he'll play. It seems safe to assume that the Knicks will have to do without the best possible Willis Reed —they will be happy with any Willis Reed at all.

The Lakers, on the other hand, finally smell a victory. Six times in the Sixties they made it to the NBA finals. Six times the Boston Celtics, led by Bill Russell, turned them back and denied them a crown. Jerry West and Elgin Baylor are getting along in years and realize that this might be their last stab at all the marbles. They are as aware as the Knicks that Oscar Robertson is playing with Lew Alcindor at Milwaukee next season, that Bob Lanier—possibly another Russell or Reed—will be teaming with those hot shooters at Detroit next season. West, Baylor, and Chamberlain want this game as badly as the Knicks do.

It is hard to be optimistic, but everybody's trying. An entire column in the *Post* today is devoted to the Knick fans, that wonderful breed that contributed heavily to Monday night's miracle and is now recalling every moment of the season, looking for what they can do to help achieve a victory. Many fans will be wearing the same clothes they wore on Monday night—this is all part of the sports superstition.

The gamblers in the Garden crowd—and there are many —probably feel more optimistic than the rest of us. The "morning line" in the *Post* shows the Knicks as 5-point favorites. The Garden gamblers are always sure that the bookies know more than the press, the fans, or even the doctors. If the Knicks are favored, then Willis will play and play well, or so the gamblers may think.

174

Cazzie Russell and Dave DeBusschere were the only bright spots for the Knicks in Wednesday's loss. Caz hit on 10-for-14 from the floor and scored 23 points in only 31 minutes. If Reed is not at top form, Caz will have to do it again and get help besides that which DeBusschere offered. Dave got hot in the second half and finished with 25 points in 36 minutes, hitting on 12-for-25. Most of those shots were perimeter jumpers on which Chamberlain refused to go out. The Knicks will need those again tonight.

No game has ever meant as much to me as tonight's game. I haven't really stopped thinking, worrying, and talking about tonight's game since the end of the first quarter on Wednesday. It's been a helluva long season and it's been full of thrills, but what went before will have a somewhat empty ring if there is no success tonight. And the Knicks know it.

My girlfriend has been bedridden with a cold for two days. She is going to drag herself out to go to the game tonight. Before this season started, she wouldn't have known Walt Frazier from Arturo Toscanini. But after one season with the Knicks, she feels their fortunes are her fortunes. I am sure she is not alone. Besides, as she pointed out, we can't expect Willis to try to play with a strained hip if she won't shrug off a cold and sore throat to go and watch.

When I sat down to tell you how it is waiting for this game, I thought I would run out of paper long before I ran out of thoughts. The game has been playing over and over in my head and we are still several hours away from the opening tip-off. Perhaps the truth is that my head has been swimming with the same thoughts, sort of like a treadmill, for the past several days. There really isn't that much more to say. Nobody seems to know for sure whether Willis Reed will play, and without him the Knicks' chances are, as they say, slim and none. The problem with Monday night's miracle is that it seems as impossible to repeat as it would if it had never happened. The Captain is the heart and soul of the Knickerbockers and—to borrow Walt Frazier's metaphor—without him the Knicks look like a sinking ship.

MAY 9

All that worrying for nothing. In a season that started with a blaze of perfection, the Knicks had one perfect record left: they had not yet lost a "must" game. The season concluded with that perfect record intact and the first NBA crown ever for New York.

The hero of the piece was Willis Reed, who last night gave one of the most couraegous performances in sports history. Clearly hobbled, unable to jump or run in even a facsimile of his normal manner, Willis still came in to do a crucial job for 27 minutes. He kept Wilt Chamberlain away from the boards, allowing the Knicks to go head-to-head with the four other Lakers. It was no contest. Only a futile rally by the Lakers, long after the issue had been decided, pulled the score to a nearly respectable 113–99. The Knicks led by 25 most of the way.

This was a one-sided basketball game, but it did not lack for drama. The Knicks had concluded their layups and were having shooting practice before the game when Reed emerged from the locker room. I had called Bob Wolff earlier in the afternoon to find out whether Willis would play and had been assured that he would at least give it a go, although nobody could know what he might be able to do. As gametime neared, however, I shared the fear that Reed's emergence, when it occurred, might be in street-clothes. But Reed came out suited up, as resplendent as one can be in the Knickerbockers' home white uniform and the crowd roared and rose. He took a shot from the lane as the crowd continued to roar, and missed. Then he popped in two from the baseline, barely leaving his feet to jump, and the roar grew.

The game started, and few fears were allayed in the opening minute. Willis was dragging, pushing himself merely to get from one end of the court to the other. The Knicks found him open on the perimeter on their first sortie and he canned the shot. The score, which gave the Knicks a 2-0 lead, seemed to put fire into the crowd and into the team. Los Angeles came back to tie it up at 2–2, but it was the only time the Lakers were to achieve a tie. Bill Bradley hit a foul shot and Reed another "jumper" to stretch the lead to 5–2 in the next minute. From there it was all downhill. Walt Frazier took over the offense, taking Laker rookie Dick Garrett for a roller-coaster ride he'll never forget. With Frazier harassing the Laker defenders, hitting 5-for-5 from both the floor and the line in the first quarter and starting on his way to a playoff-record-tying nineteen assists, the Knicks took command by 38–24 at the end of the first quarter.

Reed could not use all his physical tools, so he was concentrating on what was left to him. He used his bulk and strength to lean on Chamberlain as Wilt tried to set up on the low post. While Willis could not jump well enough to hassle Wilt when he went up to shoot, he frequently forced Chamberlain to pass off before he could make a move against Willis's immobile and unmovable frame. A corollary benefit of Reed's play, to the Knicks, was that Chamberlain held the ball much longer than he usually does. This allowed quick hands like those of Bradley, Frazier, DeBusschere, and Barnett to peck at Big Wilt from the other side, resulting in a series of turnovers.

Offensively, the shots Reed hit were vitally important, aside from the psychological lift they provided the Knicks. The fact that Reed's shooting was apparently unaffected by his layoff or his injury compelled Chamberlain to come out to guard him. Willis only attempted three more shots after the two quick ones he put in. He missed all three, but in effect it was as if he'd hit. With Chamberlain's attention drawn away from the basket, the middle was open, the baseline was open. In the first half, Frazier and Bradley particularly, took advantage of this situation to get good shots inside. In addition, Reed set crushing picks, something the Knicks sorely lacked in Wednesday's loss, to free all the deadly guns, especially DeBusschere, for the perimeter jump shots. Reed picked up his third personal late in the second quarter, so Holzman sat him down in favor of Nate Bowman. Even with Willis out, the fired-up Knicks tood advantage of the disorganized Lakers to expand their lead. Bowman, seemingly inspired by what Reed had accomplished on one leg, had his best game of the playoffs, notwithstanding the 18 points he managed on Wednesday. Nate kept Chamberlain working hard. There were few easy baskets. While we in the stands would have been happy if the Knicks had held their first-quarter lead until halftime, they nearly doubled it. At intermission the score was 69–42. The ballgame was over.

Reed again made a dramatic entry to start the second half. Although at that point I think few doubted that the Knicks would win even without Reed in the second half, we all expected him to start. He had to receive a second shot of cortisone before he continued, so he didn't come back out until after Nate Bowman had lined up for the second-half tap. The crowd rose as Reed made his way toward the Knick bench. Bill Bradley stepped into the jump circle and requested that the referees wait for Reed. They did, and Willis replaced Bowman in the circle.

The Knicks cooled off in the second half, particularly in the early stages. Bill Bradley missed three wide-open jump shots from pretty close range—unusual for him—but the Lakers were too disorganized and disheartened to capitalize. The Knick defense had not let up one iota and the Laker frustrations in shooting matched the Knicks' worst streak. One reason for this was that Jerry West must have been awfully tired. Usually the Lakers attempt to rest West in subtle ways. They don't ask him to bring the ball up and they have him guard the weaker of the two opposing guards. The Knicks' first-half press, however, ended up forcing Mullaney to have West bring up the ball. Also, Frazier's offensive heroics against Garrett necessitated that West be switched to guard him. Meanwhile, with West off him, Barnett got torrid later in the second half and provided the Knicks' offensive spark as they wrapped up the title.

The game was televised nationally. Since the New York area was blacked out, the game was shown on a delayed tape. I watched the tape and found the postgame locker-room comments of the Knicks extremely revealing. To a man, they cited two big factors that enabled the Knicks to turn around Wednesday's crushing defeat. One, of course, was the presence of Willis Reed. The other was the encouragement of the fans, constantly rabid and helpful all season but reaching new heights in the playoffs. Dave DeBusschere and Red Holzman, particularly, cited fan support as helping to make possible the Knick recovery by pumping untold quantities of extra adrenalin through their veins. "You can't play badly in front of these fans," DeBusschere said with a smile. "They just won't *let* you!" The credit the Knick players placed with the fans gives extra significance to the shouts of *"We're Number One"* that began shortly after the chant of *"It's All Over Now"* late in the fourth quarter.

The Knick fans are number one, and I must admit that

I'm proud for having been a part of it. Last night's crowd was partisan, but in good taste. Jerry West was cheered enthusiastically when he was introduced before the game, and Elgin Baylor received a standing ovation when he went out in the fourth quarter. One of the indices of the trouble this country is in is that a respect for excellence has often been subordinated to partisanship. Knick fans last night showed that you can help your side and still have respect for the accomplishments of the other. I doubt that there is a Laker player, after last night's game, who doesn't wish he played in front of people like the fans in New York.

Reed's gritty performance and the outstanding play he exhibited before he was injured earned him the MVP award for the championship round. The Knick players, to a man, gave 100 percent to contribute to last night's victory. But it may be that the final margin was provided by the ingenuity of Red Holzman and Joe Mullaney's inability to think as quickly as the Knick mentor. The Lakers, for a fleeting moment in the first half, installed Chamberlain on the high post, where he could be used to pick for Laker shooters the way Reed is used for New York. This, in the long run, could have been the Lakers' solution to the Knick problem. Reed's immobility would have hurt him badly if he had to switch quickly on Baylor, West, Erickson, or Garrett after a Chamberlain pick pulled off another Knickerbocker. As it was played, Willis's immobility hurt his performance, but he was able to compensate for it as the Laker game allowed Willis to substitute strength for speed. Holzman understood Reed's limitations and made the proper adjustments—such as having Frazier go to the basket more —to compensate for them.

It has been a wonderful season, albeit a long one. One problem with writing a book based faithfully on the true story of a basketball team is that you cannot change the story to provide dramatics. But what might have been a handicap was turned by the Knicks into an advantage. Their exciting play, balance, and collective courage assured a great measure of thrills and an ultimate success. They were truly what the New Yorker would want his basketball team to be: diverse, talented, and integrated in every way, and, most of all, intelligent. Willis Reed triumphed over the toughest parlay of matchups in the history of the playoffs—Unseld, Alcindor, and Chamberlain in succession, and his triumph was as intellectual as it was physical. Walt Frazier used psychology on defense in ways that would have made Bill Russell very proud. Dick Barnett was sage and wise, knowing when offensive spurts were needed, knowing when defensive concentration was required. Not enough can be said for the performance of Dave DeBusschere, who gave the extra effort time after time to snare a rebound, stop an opponents' drive, hit a jumper—and always at the crucial time. Bill Bradley played his game well and helped out his teammates—it should never be forgotten that Bradley conceived the 1–3–1 offense that won the fifth game.

The bench also "gave," as they had all season. Only Donnie May didn't play in the final round of the playoffs, but you somehow knew that if his contribution had been needed, it would have come. The rest of the bench provided spark in the clutch, particularly in the fifth game of the Laker series.

The entire season was, in a sense, one big show. Next year's will not be the same, even if we get the same ending. In any case, I wouldn't miss it for the world.

The Game Itself, Including Hints on Terminology

Basketball is played between two five-man teams on the floor, plus substitutes. The object of the game is to outscore the opponent by throwing a large round ball through a larger metal hoop more frequently than the opposition.

In the NBA, the game is divided into four 12-minute quarters. The 48-minute professional game is longer than the college game (two 20-minute halves) and the high school game (four 8-minute quarters). The NBA schedule consists of 82 games, plus preseason exhibitions and play-offs, which can push the total over a hundred. College seasons are a maximum of thirty games, so there is an adjustment required of first-year professionals.

To speed up play in the NBA, there is a *24-second clock*. A team is required to take a shot that at least hits either the rim or the backboard within 24 seconds of the time it gains possession of the ball. If it fails to do so, it loses possession. The purpose of this rule is to prevent a team from hanging on to a big (and sometimes not so big) lead by stalling: passing the ball around without attempting to score, holding the ball, dribbling in circles. It accomplishes that function admirably. It is not at all uncommon to see a 10- or 12-point lead vanish in a couple of minutes in a pro game.

It is uncommon in college basketball, where there is no 24-second clock. A corollary of the rule is that scores are generally much higher in the pro game.

There is a *10-second rule,* which requires that a team move the ball past the midcourt line within 10 seconds of the time they take it from out of bounds behind the baseline. Once it has crossed the midcourt line, it may not move the ball back across the line. This is a *backcourt violation.* Either a 10-second violation or a backcourt violation results in loss of possession.

The most misunderstood of the rudimentary rules in basketball is the *3-second rule.* There is an area called the *key,* or *lane,* which is an area 16-feet wide (in the NBA) and extending from under the basket to the foul line. No offensive player is permitted to be in that lane for more than 3 seconds, regardless of whether he has the ball. The key term is "offensive player." A player is on offense only if his team clearly has possession of the ball, so the 3-second rule would *not* apply after the ball is shot and it is unclear which team has possession. I can promise you that if you go to a basketball game you will hear fans yelling "3 seconds, 3 seconds" when a battle for a loose ball is going on in the lane. I can also promise you that many referees, on the professional level and below, will call the violation when it clearly could *not* have occurred, such as within a second after a missed shot. Whether he is right or wrong, however, the ref's judgment counts and a 3-second violation results in loss of possession.

A foul occurs, technically, when two opposing players come into contact. Practically speaking, the contact must affect play before a foul will be called. Otherwise, with the amount of jostling that goes on in the NBA, the referees would constantly be blowing the whistle. Most fouls are committed by the defense: holding, hacking, or bumping

183

an offensive player. If this foul is committed when the offensive player is in the process of shooting at the basket, he is awarded two shots. If the foul occurs in the backcourt, he is also awarded two shots. If the referee considers the foul "flagrant," he is awarded two shots. In all other cases, the foul is a one-shot foul. If a player is fouled while in the act of shooting and the shot is good, his basket counts and he gets a foul shot for a possible 3-*point play*.

If a foul is committed by an offensive player, there is no foul shot. The offensive team simply loses possession. An offensive foul occurs most frequently when the player who has the ball moves into a stationary defensive player.

If neither team has possession, such as on a rebound, and a foul is committed, it is a *loose-ball foul*. The NBA added this designation in the 1969–70 season. Loose-ball fouls result in the offended team taking possession, unless the offending team is *over the limit* for fouls.

Each team is permitted four fouls per quarter; they go over the limit with the fifth foul in any quarter. All fouls committed by a team count as team fouls, except *offensive fouls*, which are charged only to the player and not the team. When a team is over the limit, we have the *penalty situation*. All one-shot fouls become two, except the one shot that is awarded following a successful basket. That becomes two opportunities to make one shot. All two-shot fouls become three chances to make two points. On the college level and below, the penalty situation gives the offended team a *one-and-one*. If the foul-shooter makes the first shot, he gets a bonus.

Each player is permitted six fouls in a professional game. Upon incurring his sixth, however, he must leave the game and may not return unless injuries to teammates make it necessary. In that case, every foul he commits will be accompanied by a *technical* foul, where the opposition shoots one foul shot and can designate whatever player they want to shoot it. Technical fouls are more frequently assessed for arguing too strenuously with the referee and technical violations of the rules, such as having too many men on the court.

An NBA team is permitted to dress twelve men for each game. They are *required* to dress eight men, although no more than five need play if there is no foul trouble.

Offensive Basketball

Basketball, far more than any other team sport, is a game of offense. The frequency of scoring is unmatched in any other game, and the speed and improvisational ability required of players is matched only in ice hockey. It is literally impossible to see everything that goes on in a basketball game. If you follow the ball, you will see a great pass go to an unguarded player—and the question of how he got loose from his defender will remain unanswered. If you take your eyes off the ball to watch someone moving without it, you may miss a pass or shot. Here I will mention what goes on so that *whatever* you watch you understand what is happening.

The two men who handle the ball most on any professional basketball team are the guards. Generally speaking, they are also the shortest men on the floor and the best outside shooters, or most accurate at scoring from greater distance. It is the responsibility of the guards to "penetrate," or move the ball closer to the basket by dribbling or passing it, making it possible for their team to get "better-percentage shots", or shots closer to the basket. The general range in height of NBA guards is from 6-foot-2 to 6-foot-4. All three of the Knicks' important guards—Walt Frazier,

Dick Barnett, and Mike Riordan—are 6-foot-4 and are considered tall guards.

Generally speaking, the highest-scoring players in basketball have been the forwards. The forwards are usually taller than the guards and have the added responsibility of rebounding or returning missed shots as well as scoring. The Knick forwards are generally shorter than the opposition's. Cazzie Russell and Bill Bradley are about 6-foot-5, and Dave DeBusschere and Dave Stallworth are about 6-foot-6. Don May is an exceptionally short forward at 6-foot-4. Only Bill Hosket, at 6-foot-8, is considered a tall forward.

The center is usually the tallest man on the team. His height is frequently close to or over 7 feet although there are centers who are considerably shorter. Westley Unseld of Baltimore is an excellent center at 6-foot-8. Willis Reed is no taller than 6-foot-10. Bill Russell, the first truly great center in basketball and perhaps the greatest who ever played, was 6-foot-9. The center is frequently the hub of the offense, stationing himself with his back to the basket and as close to it as the 3-second lane will allow, enabling his teammates to move past him and around him in attempts to evade their defenders.

The most important tool in offensive basketball is the "pick," or "screen." This is accomplished when an offensive player stations himself next to the defender who is guarding a teammate. When the teammate moves he forces the man guarding him to bump into the man who set the pick, thus for a length of time he is "open." Obviously, the bigger the player setting the pick, the more effective it becomes. One of Willis Reed's strongest assets is that he can set a pick at some distance from the basket while being fast enough to get to the basket to contest the rebound of a shot.

When a player sets a pick, the defender who is guarding him is often in a good position to guard the offensive player moving off the pick who might otherwise be freed. When this happens, the man who set the pick might move quickly to the basket, now unguarded, to receive a pass for an easy shot. Again, Willis Reed's speed enables him to do this very well.

All professional basketball players are good shooters, and all will score on a high percentage of shots taken within 15 feet of the basket. Some, however, are very effective from a greater distance. Dick Barnett and Dave DeBusschere have the longest range of the Knick starters, with Cazzie Russell providing long-distance firepower from the bench. All three of these men are dangerous up to 25 feet from the basket. Obviously, the threat of their ability to shoot from a long distance forces the opposition defense to spread itself over a larger area, making more room for the other Knick players to get good shots from closer range.

There are "set plays" in basketball, as there are in football, but they are not used every time a team comes up the floor. On these set plays, a shot might be taken at various times. The advantage of a set play is that the man with the ball has a good idea where and when it is most likely that a teammate will become open.

Essentially, there are two styles of offensive basketball: the "fast break" and the "deliberate." A fast-breaking style, having the offense move down the floor as quickly as it can, often results in easy baskets—such as when the players on the offensive team get into the forecourt and outnumber the defenders, or when the defenders who are back are equal in number but are not the players who customarily guard the fast-breakers. It is frequently advantageous to the offense to create these "mismatches," since a taller defender might be considerably slower than a quick guard or a shorter defender might have trouble with a tall forward. The mismatches created by a fast-break offense often last until the offensive play is completed, since even when all ten players are up the floor there might not be an advantageous time for the defense to switch back to their normal assignment without leaving a man open. The danger in fast-breaking is that the ball can be thrown away or fumbled while moving at great speed. The Knicks employ a fast-break offense most of the time, having guards of superior ballhandling ability and forwards who handle the ball considerably better than most.

Deliberate basketball is accomplished by allowing the entire offense to set up in position, even though this allows the defense extra time. A team might play deliberately because of a deficiency—such as a lack of ballhandling ability by its guards—or to employ a strength—such as the superior height of its forwards. When the forwards on offense are much taller than their opponents, it is frequently an advantage to have everybody participate in the offense, since it is not difficult to get a great number of offensive rebounds.

In the NBA, the Knicks and Atlanta Hawks are the premier examples of the fast-break offense, and the Los Angeles Lakers, Philadelphia 76ers, and San Francisco Warriors are noted for their deliberate style.

The biggest "no-no" in offensive basketball is to commit a "turnover," loss of the ball without attempting a shot. It is caused by an offensive foul, traveling (moving with the ball without dribbling), throwing the ball away, or allowing a defender to take it away, usually during a dribble.

There are essentially two different types of offensive ballplayers: those who move well *without* the ball, and those who move well *with* the ball. There are players who do both, such as Frazier and Jerry West, but most are more effective one way or the other. Bill Bradley is one of the best players in the league at moving without the ball and getting free to receive a pass. Dave Bing of Detroit is much

188

more effective *with* the ball. It is important to remember that all the offensive maneuvers—faking a defender or using a pick, for example—can be done even by a player without the ball. Particularly when a team has a good passer like Frazier or Len Wilkins, it doesn't matter whether the player who gets open has the ball. If he does not have it, a good passer will get it to him.

The shooting in professional basketball has improved markedly in the past decade. When Ken Sears of the Knicks shot about .500 about ten years ago (that is, sank about 50 percent of the shots he attempted from the "floor," as opposed to the foul line), it was considered absolutely remarkable shooting. Today, all of the top ten shooters in the NBA are over .500, and not all of them are forwards and centers, who take shots from close to the basket. Jon McGlocklin of Milwaukee, Lou Hudson of Atlanta, Dick Snyder of Seattle, and Frazier are all in the top ten and are guards.

From the foul line the percentages are much higher. Flynn Robinson is the top foul-shooter in the NBA, hitting on nearly 90 percent. A team should shoot better than 70 percent from the foul line and upward of 40 percent from the floor. Foul-shooting of over 80 percent or floor-shooting of over 50 percent indicates a superior marksman.

There are certain things to watch for that indicate a good offensive ballplayer. Obviously, his ability to score—both when left open and under defensive pressure—is important. But you must also watch how well he handles the ball. Can he make progress in getting closer to the basket when he is guarded? Does he successfully pass the ball to a teammate who gets open? Does he set picks for his teammates? Does he assist the offense by moving to get open or to help a teammate get open when he does *not* have the ball?

There is one more important offensive factor, but it is

an "intangible." Offensive basketball relies heavily on "momentum" for movement, passing, shooting. A player who holds the ball for a great length of time on offense, particularly when his teammates have been doing a lot of passing, can spoil the momentum of an offense. Let me emphasize that it is not important whether that player ultimately scores or passes for a score on a particular occasion when he controlled the ball. He may still have hurt his team's momentum. There are some ballplayers who are relied upon to control the ball a great deal of the time as an integral part of the team's offensive plan. Walt Frazier and Oscar Robertson are the best examples of this type of player. Nonetheless, both know when *not* to hold the ball or slow the tempo if the offensive rhythm will suffer.

If nothing else is clear from these pages, it should be obvious that the offense has many tools with which to score. All NBA teams average well over 100 points per game. Nonetheless, defense is as important a part to a winning effort as is offense, although it is not as obvious. Let us examine the defense.

Defensive Basketball

There are two basic types of defense—zone and man-to-man. In zone defense, each defender is responsible for covering an area of the floor. In man-to-man, each defender guards a specific opponent wherever he goes. Zone defense is outlawed in the NBA. The reason for this is that it cuts down on "driving," or dribbling toward the basket, for a score. It is more difficult to drive against a zone because the offensive player will be picked up by a new defender. It is not necessarily more difficult to *score* against a zone, but driving is an exciting part of basketball.

There are many things that a coach must consider when he decides on his *matchups* in man-to-man defense. Frequently, a player who is counted upon heavily for an offensive contribution will not be asked to guard a difficult opponent, regardless of his ability to do well. Playing an easier opponent on defense diminishes the possibility that our offensive star will get into foul trouble and cuts down on his expenditure of energy. Generally, one of the forwards of a basketball team will take the toughest opposition forward and a particular guard will take the toughest guard. Generally on the Knicks, Dave DeBusschere takes the difficult forward assignment and Dick Barnett the difficult guard, for different reasons.

Dave DeBusschere is one of the top defensive forwards in the NBA. He has all the physical requisites and has concentrated on defense, so he has the know-how and determination to guard an Elgin Baylor, Gus Johnson, and Billy Cunningham. Dave is important to the Knick offense, but not as indispensable as are Frazier and Reed, for example. The only forwards who are as capable defensively as Debusschere are Gus Johnson and, perhaps, Satch Sanders.

Walt Frazier may well be the top defensive guard in the league, but he is not usually assigned the top opponent man-to-man. There are several reasons for this. First of all, Frazier is critically important to the New York offense, so his energy and fouls may not be lightly sacrificed. Secondly, Frazier is so quick that he is frequently able to help out a teammate on defense if his primary responsibility is not against a superstar. When he does leave his man to help out a teammate, or double-team, the rest of the Knick offense must adjust to the possibility that he might not get back to his man before the ball does. So there is a risk, but all the Knicks are so alert that the risk is minimized.

Starting at a young age, neophyte basketball players are taught to guard their opponents at a distance of about 3 feet, and to always stay between their opponent and the basket. This is a technique that the Knicks do not usually employ. The Knick defense is a "ball-hawking" defense that concentrates on forcing turnovers, and they generally play between their man and the ball rather than between their man and the basket. Bill Bradley is the master of this style of defense, which requires a constant computation of the changing angles caused by the movement of the ball and the opponent. Bradley can often shut off much taller opponents by making it almost impossible for them to get the ball. If he fails at this initial deterrent he can be in serious trouble, as many tall forwards can shoot over Bradley. But first they must get the ball.

Neophyte basketball players are also taught to guard their opponent on the opponent's stronger side. That is, if DeBusschere is guarding Bailey Howell, he would (with this theory) overguard to Howell's right, since Howell is righthanded and would prefer to move and shoot to the right. In practice, the opponent's strength is one of a number of factors that governs how he is guarded. With the Knicks' emphasis on team defense, and "helping out," an opponent might be overplayed to encourage him to drive toward another defender. Depending on the strategy employed at a specific time against a specific team or player, he might be overguarded to be encouraged to drive toward the middle or the sideline. In any case, you can be sure that whatever overguarding occurs is by predesign and part of an overall team concept of how an opponent is to be defensed.

A strong, quick center like Willis Reed can be an important part of a defense. Reed's ability to "switch off" his own man to pick up a driving opponent allows the other

Knicks to attempt steals and other defensive maneuvers at the risk of allowing their man to drive by them. Bill Russell changed the entire concept of defense by his ability to clog up the middle of the floor near the basket by switching off his man to cover another. Obviously, the offense will attempt to counter this by passing the ball to the man newly unguarded, but this is not easy to do against a 6-foot-10 or 7-foot center.

The cardinal rule of playing defense is not to cross the legs when moving with an opponent. Rather, a "shuffle step" should be used in order to maintain better balance and change direction. Nonetheless, you will see players in the NBA who frequently cross their legs on defense.

While zone defense is illegal in the NBA, certain hybrids containing elements of a zone are used. One is the "zone press." This is a defensive maneuver that challenges the offense from the time it takes the ball from out of bounds after a basket by covering the entire length and width of the floor. This is a dangerous strategy, since a series of quick passes can frequently give the offense an easy basket, so it is usually employed as a desperation measure, such as when a team is far behind late in a game.

Another hybrid is often employed against the Milwaukee Bucks, who have Lew Alcindor at center but forwards who are not good outside shooters. When Alcindor, almost impossible to stop one-on-one, stations himself with his back to the basket ("low post"), the forward who is guarding an opponent on the same side will often drop back to "front" Lew, conceding a 15- to 20-foot shot to his opponent. If Milwaukee were to come up with a forward who was an outside scoring threat, he would make Lew that much more effective. The defender guarding the new Milwaukee forward would have to stay out on him, making it easier to get the ball to Lew. By the same token, the presence of

Alcindor made guard Flynn Robinson a more effective scorer. Offenses used to gang up on Robinson outside, but they couldn't do that with the threat of Alcindor.

Rebounding is really part of offensive basketball too, but it is crucial to good defense. The important first step of rebounding is to "box out," or "block off," an opponent by planting oneself as widely as possible between him and the backboard. Once boxing out is accomplished, it is much easier to get the rebound. A forward like Bill Bradley does not get many rebounds, due to his tremendous height disadvantage. On the other hand, Bradley boxes out so well that he neutralizes a taller opponent, thus making it easier for Reed and DeBusschere to get the ball.

These pages do not tell you everything you need to know to fully understand basketball. But if you keep in mind the items that are covered here, you will have an essential grasp of what's going on and enough knowledge to question the judgment of referees, sportscasters, and coaches. Basketball appears at first glance to be considerably less complex than it is, which may be why so many sportscasters and fans speak authoratatively—and mistakenly—about it. If some of what appears in these pages is new to you—and you thought you knew the game—don't be intimidated. The emotional involvement of the fan that makes him scream at officials and second-guess coaches supplies at least half the fun. And it may well be that looking at it from your perch, you might even want to second-guess or scream at me.

The League Structure

The *National Basketball Association* is basketball's established "major league." There is a new league, the *American Basketball Association* (ABA), which is attempting to establish itself as a league of equal status by competing with the NBA for the graduating college seniors and, at times, enticing NBA ballplayers to "jump" to the ABA. In 1960 the American Football League was established and challenged the National Football League in the same manner, and the AFL was successful and eventually forced a merger. It is unclear whether the ABA will have the same measure of success, as it does not have the support of a national-television contract as did the AFL. But there is a merger committee for each league and the two are discussing the possibilities.

The NBA is divided into two divisions, Western and Eastern, with seven teams in each division. The West contains the San Diego Rockets, Los Angeles Lakers, San Francisco Warriors, Seattle SuperSonics, Phoenix Suns, Chicago Bulls, and Atlanta Hawks. In the East are the Knicks, the Boston Celtics, Baltimore Bullets, Philadelphia 76ers, Detroit Pistons, Cincinnati Royals, and the Milwaukee Bucks. At the end of the league season, the playoffs in the NBA determine the "world champion." In each division, the first-place and third-place finishers play a best-of-seven series, as do the second- and fourth-place teams. (The teams that finish fifth, sixth, and last in each division do not qualify for the playoffs.) The winners of the two preliminary series in each division play a best-of-seven series for the divisional championship; then the two divisional champs meet in a best-of-seven series for the world championship. (The divisional structure of the NBA will change with the addition of three new teams for the 1970–71 season.)

The NBA has a lucrative television contract with ABC-Television, and the money it receives, plus the weekly exposure, has supplied a stability that did not always exist. For example, the Detroit Pistons started in Fort Wayne, Indiana, and the Los Angeles Lakers in Minneapolis. The most recent franchise shift occurred when the Hawks moved from St. Louis to Atlanta before the 1967–68 season. When the Hawks first came into existence, they played in Milwaukee.

The league has been adding teams at a rapid rate during the past decade, having most recently added Milwaukee and Phoenix during the 1968–69 season. There is additional expansion scheduled before the 1970–71 season, with three new teams to be added.

At the conclusion of each NBA season, there is a "draft" of the rights to graduating college seniors. In this draft, the teams pick in the order of finish, with the last-place teams picking first. The losers in the West and East participate in a coin-toss to determine which of them will start the draft. A drafted college player must sign with the team that drafted him (or sign with the ABA) if he wants to play professional basketball. The draft is a critical element of the attempts to maintain balance in the league, since the teams with the worst records get the best opportunties to strengthen themselves. Sometimes one solid ballplayer can revitalize a whole team. The Baltimore Bullets finished last in the East in 1967–68 and drafted Westley Unseld of Louisville. With Unseld they finished first. The Milwaukee Bucks finished last in 1968–69 and drafted Lew Alcindor, who moved the team up to second place.

THE BOSTON CELTICS. Before the 1969–70 season, the Boston Celtics had won the world championship eleven times in thirteen years. For the thirteen seasons preceding 1969–70, their center was Bill Russell. And those championship teams were built around him.

Offensively, the Celtics used their center to create shots for their good outside shooters. Sam Jones, one of them, retired with Russell, but John Havlicek, Larry Siegfried,

Don Nelson, and Bailey Howell remained this year. But without Russell to move the ball from a low post and set picks farther outside, their game was severely hampered. The Celtics also used to score frequently on offensive rebounds while Mr. Russell tied up two or three of the opposition on the boards, sometimes leaving Howell or Nelson or Havlicek pretty much alone for easy shots. The Celtic fast break, formerly triggered by Russell's great defensive rebounding, also suffered.

Defensively, the Celtics' overguarded their men outside, conceding the drive to the middle, where Russell was capable of blocking shots and passes, making the "successful" penetration unsuccessful. But without Russell, the Boston defenders had to be "honest," guarding their men with the idea that there would be no help from behind if the offense elected to drive. The loss of Bill Russell affected every player on the club, offensively and defensively, and it was no surprise that the Celtics finished sixth in the division this year. Even with fine young players like Don Chaney and Jo-Jo White, the road back to the top will be a long one.

THE PHILADELPHIA 76ERS. This is a team with two great offensive ballplayers, Billy Cunningham at forward and Hal Greer at guard. The center, Darrall Imhoff, is used primarily to set picks outside, even though he is not as quick at rolling off the pick to the basket as is Willis Reed or was Bill Russell. Greer has been slowed somewhat by old age and injuries, but is a deadly jump-shooter from almost anywhere on the floor and has such capable running mates (Archie Clark and Wally Jones) that the defense cannot double-team him too often. Jim Washington, the forward opposite Cunningham, is a fair shooter and a good defensive player and rebounder.

Philadelphia frequently will clear one side for Cunningham to work one-on-one against his defender. Also as an aid to Cunningham, Imhoff rarely sets up on the low post on the same side Cunningham is playing, giving Billy more room to maneuver.

Defensively, Philadelphia is not a strong team. Cunningham is prone to foul trouble, the guards—though quick—are short, and Imhoff does not have the defensive ability to intimidate opponents who drive the lane.

THE BALTIMORE BULLETS. Baltimore is one of the most talented and deepest teams in basketball. Their starting five is a match for any in the league, and they have maintained a strength on the bench that ranks with the Knicks' as the best in the league.

The keys to the Baltimore attack are the center, Westley Unseld, and their star guard, Earl (the Pearl) Monroe. Unseld is a great rebounder and adds to his value by getting the ball to an "outlet" man, or teammate free of the traffic under the boards, very quickly after a defensive rebound. This keys the Baltimore fast break, the heart of their offense. Jack Marin, Gus Johnson, and either Kevin Loughery or Fred Carter—the starters with Monroe and Unseld—are all very quick and good shooters.

When Baltimore fails to make the fast break work, it relies primarily on Monroe or Johnson. Both are great one-on-one players. Unseld is effective at creating movement and setting picks and screens, but his primary offensive contribution at either end of the court is under the boards.

Defensively, the Bullets are also strong. Monroe has arthritic knees and tends to relax on defense somewhat, but he is not by any means helpless against opposition guards. Carter is a talented defensive player, Loughery a seasoned and intelligent one. Johnson is, with DeBusschere and Satch Sanders, one of the top defensive forwards in the league, and Unseld is excellent defensively. Only Jack Marin is not

198

top-notch on the Bullets' front line, and he is more than adequate.

THE MILWAUKEE BUCKS. This is Lew Alcindor's team. He is the heart of the offense, the essence of the defense, the bulwark of the rebounding. Greg Smith and Bob Dandridge, the starters at forward, are good rebounders but leave much to be desired offensively. Dandridge has shown signs of offensive potential, but Smith just simply is not a very good shooter. Len Chappell, a substitute forward, is, but his shortcomings on defense cannot be ignored. Obtaining Oscar Robertson to team with Jon McGlocklin at guard will make Alcindor even more effective.

The Bucks rely on Alcindor defensively the way the Celtics used to count on Bill Russell. They play an aggressive man-to-man, shutting off outside shots and counting on Alcindor to stop the drives. Smith is a very good jumper and also helps clog up the inside on defense and gives Alcindor able assistance under the boards. If Milwaukee were to come up with one first-rate pro forward, they would be almost unbeatable. As it stands, they're pretty tough.

THE CINCINNATI ROYALS. For years the Royals just "let Oscar do it." Oscar Robertson, the Big O, is one of the greatest ballplayers ever to step on the hardwood, but he never led Cincinnati to championship contention. His ability to control the tempo of the game, score among the top five in the league, pass like a magician, and penetrate the defense better than any player who ever lived, was simply not sufficient. For one thing, the other Royal ballplayers were not always "in the game." Without the ball, they tended to stand around on offense, and movement is the essential of a good, balanced offense.

This year, Bob Cousy—in his first year as coach—attempted to change the Royals' style. He traded away Jerry Lucas, the forecourt star who was sort of a junior partner in a dynamic duo with Robertson. Cousy tried to have more players handle the ball, not just Oscar. The results are difficult to analyze. The Royals lost a lot of games, but they may yet profit from the change. A rookie, Norm van Lier, and two veterans, Tom Van Arsdale and Johnny Green, all had much better seasons than anyone anticipated. The Royals received Flynn Robinson for Oscar, and it remains to be seen if Cousy will be able to mold a successful team next year along the lines he wants.

THE DETROIT PISTONS. Detroit finished last in the Eastern Division this year and assured themselves of being near the top of the league next year. They drafted and signed Bob Lanier, the top college player in the country, who, at 6-foot-11 and 275 pounds, might become as great a pro as Wilt Chamberlain, Bill Russell, or Lew Alcindor.

Jimmy Walker and Dave Bing are two of the top guards in pro ball, but Detroit is handicapped because both must have the ball to be most effective. Both are fabulous one-on-one players. Bing has threatened a jump to Washington of the ABA, but this is a year away in any case and could be nullified if the leagues merge.

Erwin Mueller and Terry Dischinger have been Detroit's top forwards. Dischinger was a great scorer in college and in his earlier pro years, but a layoff in the army seems to have hurt him. Mueller is a sharp interior passer and adequate rebounder and defensive player but not much of a scoring threat.

This will all change next year. Bill van Breda Kolff is an excellent coach—it was he who devised the strategy of splitting the guards wide against the Knicks and running the man Frazier guards away from the ball, and every coach in the league emulated it in some form. With Lanier to work around and a stable of good outside shooters, Detroit will be a factor in the years to come.

THE ATLANTA HAWKS. Atlanta won the Western Division this year and should be even stronger next, thanks to the signing of Pete Maravich. With Walt Hazzard and Lou Hudson in the backcourt, the Hawks already had great speed and shooting ability. Forward Joe Caldwell has exceptional scoring ability and is a top-notch defensive player. Caldwell can also play guard. Bill Bridges, Atlanta's answer to Gus Johnson and Dave DeBusschere, is strong and reliable at forward, works the boards extremely well, plays good defense, and is generally unappreciated around the league. Walt Bellamy did well at center for the Hawks since they obtained him from Detroit on February 1. Jim Davis, the center before Bellamy arrived, can spell at forward and guard.

With Maravich, the Hawks have a draft choice who will fit into their style of play. They run hard and fast, shoot well and often. Their defense is a tough man-to-man, with less double-teaming than the Knicks'. Now that they have Maravich, they may decide to trade Hazzard, Hudson, or Caldwell for a top-flight center (like Elvin Hayes of San Diego). Regardless, the Hawks will be a better team next year than they are now. Their shooters are unmatched, and with two great defensive players like Bridges and Caldwell they qualify as a good defensive team.

THE LOS ANGELES LAKERS. What the Lakers will be in years to come depends on Chamberlain, Baylor, and West staying active and healthy. With all three in the line-up, they play deliberate offense, using Chamberlain to set picks high or as a passing pivot down deep. West is still the

201

nonpareil shooter in the NBA, and when Chamberlain was hurt, Jerry carried the load as the Lakers shifted to a quicker-paced offense that allowed West to get the shot off before the defense got set. Happy Hairston provides strong support at forward and 1969-70 rookie Willie McCarter is a good sub guard. The re-acquisition of Gail Goodrich to play opposite West is a helpful addition, but the team's fate depends critically on three old (by basketball standards) men. If one goes the Lakers are still contenders. If they lose two, they will have to start a modified rebuilding. If all three should retire in the next season or two, the Lakers will find out how the Celtics feel without Russell and Jones.

THE CHICAGO BULLS. The Bulls made the playoffs in 1969-70 with top scoring from their forwards (Chet Walker and Bob Love), great coaching by Dick Motta, and mirrors. Their center, Tom Boerwinkle, is still outclassed by most of his opposition, but he shoots well and tries to compensate for his liabilities by setting picks and hustling all the time. Jerry Sloan was hurt for much of 1969-70, but the big guard is an important player to Chicago—top-notch defender, good ballhandler and shooter. Clem Haskins played alongside Sloan at guard but he has been traded away, leaving the Bulls a gap to fill.

The Bulls hope that Shaler Halimon, picked up from the 76ers in the trade that shifted Walker to Chicago, will also become an NBA star. Barring this, the Bulls are still a bit away from being a top-flight team. The Bulls' deliberate game is keyed to the outside shooting of Walker and Love's ability on tip-ins and offensive rebounds.

THE PHOENIX SUNS. They're getting better and should keep doing so with the great Connie Hawkins to build around. Hawkins can play either center or forward at

6-foot-8. He has great moves and agility and a confounding variety of shots and passes. Wth Paul Silas, Neal Walk, and Jerry Chambers in the forward slots with him, the Suns have good strength under the boards. Dick Van Arsdale and Art Harris are the starting guards. Both drive well and are better-than-average outside shooters and ballhandlers.

The Suns battled the Lakers to seven games in the 1969-70 Western Division semi-final. With another year of playing together—particularly for Hawkins, who was not used to the NBA—they should achieve natural improvement. The ability to put the ball in the hoop is there. With better work on defense and under the boards, the Suns could be one of the league's better teams. The manpower is there.

THE SAN DIEGO ROCKETS. The Rockets are in great flux due to apparent personality problems between forward Don Kojis and center Elvin Hayes. When Hayes and Kojis are healthy and happy and teamed with 6-foot-10 John Block up front, the San Diego front line is one of the league's best. First-draft-choice Rudy Tomjanovich of Michigan is a strong forward and should help there, making one of the holdover forwards available for trade for a guard.

Stu Lantz was the top Rocket guard, with Bernie Williams, Art Williams, and Pat Riley also in the San Diego backcourt. Ballhandling and defense were the Rockets' biggest problems. The acquisition of Larry Siegfried, solid guard—will improve this team.

San Diego has employed a fairly deliberate offense, working primarily to Block and Hayes and attempting to use the strong front line to get second and third shots. A strong rebounding team can also go to the fast break if they have the manpower at guard. What San Diego will be like next season depends on what else is cooked up in the trade market this summer.

THE SAN FRANCISCO WARRIORS. This team owns the rights to Nate Thurmond, Zelmo Beatty, and Rick Barry. Thurmond says he will retire and Beatty and Barry seem to be destined to play in the ABA. If any one of them plays for the Warriors next year, they will be tough. Otherwise . . .

Jerry Lucas at forward and Clyde Lee at center are good rebounders, but both are terribly slow. Lucas shoots well, as does forward Joe Ellis, who can be terrifying to the opposition when he gets hot. Jeff Mullins is a high-scoring guard who has improved his ballhandling to the point that he is one of the best in the league. Ron Williams at guard is a good ballhandler and very quick.

The Warriors are forced to play a deliberate offense because of their lack of speed up front and the necessity of using their rebounding power. If Thurmond reconsiders his retirement the team will be a good one, as Thurmond is one of the best all-around centers in basketball history. Having him in the lane to block shots makes a bad defense a good one, makes rebounding possible even with the forwards released (allowing the fast break). On offense he adds punch in the center, making it much easier for Mullins and Williams to drive without being picked up by the opposing center.

THE SEATTLE SUPERSONICS. Bob Rule, the Seattle center, is a good scorer but has trouble on defense and rebounding. And this is the team's trouble. Bob Boozer and Tom Meschery are old and wise, but the "old" also means *slow*, and knowing where you should be doesn't do you much good if you don't have the speed to get there. Wilkins is a sharp passer and a moderate offensive threat at guard, and Dick Snyder, who also starts at guard, is a good shooter.

Seattle has two possibilities for immediate improvement.

One is Rule, who seems to have the physical tools (agility, quickness, spring) to be a better all-around center than he's been. The second is Lucius Allen, formerly of UCLA, who flashed brilliantly at times during his rookie season but who could lift the team greatly if he continues to develop.

Seattle tries to compensate for its lack of speed by playing a switching man-to-man and a deliberate offense. Len Wilkins apparently held the players' respect as a player-coach during a losing season. This indicates that with the right material he could be a winning coach. But it may be a while before he has the right material.